The world we live in has thrown us a curveball, and most of us feel apprehensive. It points us to the Psalms. Weaving profound biblical truth with poignant illustration of clinging to Scripture, being intentional in our praise, reflecting on His truth, del covering our joy. You can use this resource for personal study, but even better, gather your friends—in person or screen—where you can experience transformation together.

CAROL KENT, speaker and author, *He Holds My Hand: Experiencing God's Presence and Protection*

Author Becky Harling has given us a precious gift in her latest Bible study, *The Extraordinary Power of Praise*. This study takes the reader to the feet of Jesus and equips them to receive His promise of peace in these extraordinary times. I've already taped quotes to my own bathroom mirror to remind me of God's provision. This is a book I'll share again and again.

EDIE MELSON, award-winning author and director of the Blue Ridge Mountains Christian Writers Conference

Holding this study book in my hand invites me into a sacred place with eager anticipation and poised pen. The beauty and layout of the book draws me in, but it's the honesty and authenticity of the author that spurs me on to dig deeper for those truths I desperately need. Each Morning Prayer prepares me to plumb the depths of God's love and discover necessary biblical truths. Becky writes from the heart and helps us discover the power of praise because she has lived this. We all need these tools of praise to help us break through the insidious barriers of anxiety.

HEIDI MCLAUGHLIN, international speaker and author of *Fresh Joy: Finding Joy in the Midst of Loss, Hardship and Suffering*

Becky's perspective on anxiety and worry is one we can all relate to. She beautifully leads us to God's Word and praise to renew our minds and settle our hearts on the truths about God that we can often forget during times of stress or anxiety. Through the practices of praise, memorizing God's Word, and dwelling on the truths we read about before our head hits the pillow, she helps the reader by giving them a plan to implement these practices in their everyday lives. I believe her encouragement and teaching will help us all let the peace of Christ rule in our hearts more fully as we focus our hearts toward Him.

REBECCA DOTSON GEORGE, speaker, writer, and host of the *Do The Thing Movement* podcast

The Extraordinary Power of Praise is . . . extraordinary! Becky combines solid Bible teaching with personal anecdotes to help readers understand and apply the power and principles of praise to their lives. The easy-to-follow format includes personal growth questions, space for readers to write prayers to God, a suggested Scripture memory verse, and the title of a worship song that complements the day's study. In a world filled with fear, this resource aligns readers' thoughts with God's truth and leads to life transformation. I highly recommend it for both personal and small group study.

GRACE FOX, author of *Moving from Fear to Freedom: A Woman's Guide to Peace in Every Situation*

As someone who struggles with anxiety and often feels helpless about it, Becky's newest book is pure gold! More than a Bible study, Becky's book is like an understanding-filled anxiety rehab program that kicks in the first few pages. Not only did I feel more peace while reading it, but I also felt hopeful that an anxiety-free future can be a reality. With these tools, I know it's possible. This book is a must-read for anyone who needs a little more peace and freedom in their lives!

ANNE WATSON, Business Strategy Coach

I have a tremendous amount of love and adoration for Becky. I remember asking her how she so quickly wrote *Psalms for the Anxious Heart* in the middle of a pandemic! I recall her saying that the devotional was an overflow of how she lives her life. An outpouring resulting from being in God's Word and putting it into practice. That devotional really ministered to my heart and the many I gifted it to. *The Extraordinary Power of Praise* is no different. I have read through the Psalms many times over the years, yet struggled with how to fully engage the Psalms with vulnerability before a holy God. Can I really be honest with God? The answer is yes. If you desire greater intimacy with God, a heart transformed, a mind renewed, strengthened, and refreshed, *The Extraordinary Power of Praise* is your perfect companion.

LISA BISHOP, director of Women's Ministry, Park Community Church, Chicago

Oh, friend! If you have ever spent one sleepless night in worry, if anxiety has ever run away with your joy, if you have ever been overcome by concern over the unanswered questions of life, you must absorb the truth and the hope that is lavishly given in Becky Harling's new book, *The Extraordinary Power of Praise*. This is the book that we all need to read as we process the events in our world today. Becky has accurately, practically, and hopefully communicated the eternal treasure that is brimming over in the book of Psalms. Becky has truly hit the mother lode of untapped power from this vital book in Scripture. I will be reading this book over and over again as I continue to tap into the power that is mine as I worship the Lord!

CAROL MCLEOD, blogger, podcaster, Bible teacher, writer, bestselling author of *Significant* and *Vibrant*

As Christians, we know we're supposed to "cast all your anxiety on him because he cares for you" (1 Peter 5:7), but unfortunately, that's often easier said than done—especially when we're right in the midst of our trials. I love how Becky calls us back to God's Word to find real peace, rest, and reassurance no matter what we're facing today. If you struggle with worry or anxiety, this Bible study is for you!

BRITTANY ANN, author of *Fall in Love with God's Word: Practical Strategies for Busy Women* and founder of EquippingGodlyWomen.com

As a fellow lover of the Psalms, I want to thank Becky Harling for writing *The Extraordinary Power of Praise*. It is a precious and powerful resource packed with prayers, praises, personal stories of inspiration PLUS a unique and wonderful process of using the Psalms to turn anxiety into awesome inner strength. I found myself looking forward to writing in the journaling sections because the results were peace, hope, and joy. I highly recommend this journey to all who want to learn the delight of living in serenity and strength.

PAM FARREL, bestselling author of fifty-two books, including *Discovering Hope in the Psalms: A Creative Bible Study Experience* and *Men Are Like Waffles—Women Are Like Spaghetti*

The Extraordinary Power of Praise is the perfect prescription for the difficult times we are living in. In its pages, you will find peace, comfort, and hope as you dig into God's Word and the truths that Becky shares each day. Her journey of learning to praise even in the most difficult circumstances will inspire your faith and ignite a new passion in you to follow Jesus with praise in your heart and on your lips. You will want to make time and space to ponder each day's questions and to reflect and meditate on the Scriptures Becky shares, so this study goes deep into your heart and makes a lasting impact.

KRISTIN LEMUS, founder of Brave Moms, speaker, and podcast host

When I opened Becky Harling's book *The Extraordinary Power of Praise*, I was literally drowning in my own personal fear and sorrow. From the very first page, God began to lift my heart and change my attitude. I began listening to precious YouTube praise music. I started printing out verses from the Psalms and putting them around house, and journaling my prayers. I woke with praise on my lips and went to sleep praising God. When fear started to creep in, I wept before the Lord and shared all with Him and ended with praise. I have made a Thankful List, and so much more. All of these precious experiences were encouraged and directed by Harling in her powerful book, *The Extraordinary Power of Praise*. I am so grateful. Thousands of others need this book as well.

JENNIE AFMAN DIMKOFF, author and international speaker, Global Board Member, ODB Ministries

THE EXTRAORDINARY POWER OF

PRAISE

A Study of the Psalms for the Anxious Heart

BECKY HARLING

MOODY PUBLISHERS

CHICAGO

All Scripture quotations, unless otherwise indicated, are taken from the Holy Bible, New International Version®, NIV®. Copyright © 1973, 1978, 1984, 2011 by Biblica, Inc.™ Used by permission of Zondervan. All rights reserved worldwide. www.zondervan.com The "NIV" and "New International Version" are trademarks registered in the United States Patent and Trademark Office by Biblica, Inc.™

Scripture quotations marked NLT are taken from the Holy Bible, New Living Translation, copyright ©1996, 2004, 2015 by Tyndale House Foundation. Used by permission of Tyndale House Publishers, a Division of Tyndale House Ministries, Carol Stream, Illinois 60188. All rights reserved.

All emphasis in Scripture has been added.

Published in association with the literary agency of The Blythe Daniel Agency, Inc., P.O. Box 64197, Colorado Springs, CO 80962-4197.

Edited by Amanda Cleary Eastep
Interior and cover design: Kaylee Lockenour
Cover illustration of background painting copyright © 2019 by SantaLiza / Shutterstock (772039342). All rights reserved.

All websites and phone numbers listed herein are accurate at the time of publication but may change in the future or cease to exist. The listing of website references and resources does not imply publisher endorsement of the site's entire contents. Groups and organizations are listed for informational purposes, and listing does not imply publisher endorsement of their activities.

Library of Congress Cataloging-in-Publication Data

Names: Harling, Becky, 1957- author.
Title: The extraordinary power of praise : a study of the Psalms for the
  anxious heart / Becky Harling.
Description: Chicago : Moody Publishers, [2021] | Includes bibliographical
  references. | Summary: "The Extraordinary Power of Praise will help you
  put into practice the two-step process for soothing an anxious heart:
  finding joy to replace anxiety and learning to pour out our hearts to
  God in praise. Each day of this 8-week study includes a study of a
  Psalm, thought-provoking questions, and short morning and evening
  prayers"-- Provided by publisher.
Identifiers: LCCN 2020057841 (print) | LCCN 2020057842 (ebook) | ISBN
  9780802420091 (paperback) | ISBN 9780802498915 (ebook)
Subjects: LCSH: Bible. Psalms--Criticism, interpretation, etc. |
  Anxiety--Religious aspects--Christianity.
Classification: LCC BV4908.5 .H3458 2021 (print) | LCC BV4908.5 .H3458
  2021 (ebook) | DDC 223/.206--dc23
LC record available at https://lccn.loc.gov/2020057841
LC ebook record available at https://lccn.loc.gov/2020057842

Originally delivered by fleets of horse-drawn wagons, the affordable paperbacks from D. L. Moody's publishing house resourced the church and served everyday people. Now, after more than 125 years of publishing and ministry, Moody Publishers' mission remains the same—even if our delivery systems have changed a bit. For more information on other books (and resources) created from a biblical perspective, go to www.moodypublishers.com or write to:

Moody Publishers
820 N. LaSalle Boulevard
Chicago, IL 60610

1 3 5 7 9 10 8 6 4 2

Printed in the United States of America

This book is dedicated

to our precious daughter, Keri!

Nothing delights my heart more

than hearing you lead worship.

You are a gift!

Love you so much!

Becky Harling's devotional book *Psalms for the Anxious Heart: A 30-Day Devotional for Uncertain Times* (Moody Publishers) serves as a powerful companion piece to this Bible study. Visit moodypublishers.com.

CONTENTS

INTRODUCTION

For Your Anxious Heart

For as far back as I can remember, I've struggled with anxiety. I'm pretty sure I was a neurotic little kid who worried about a whole lot of stuff. I worried about my friends—had they accepted Jesus into their hearts, and would they go to heaven? I worried about my family—would they die and leave me all alone? I worried about suffering for my faith in Jesus—would I be brave enough? I know. Neurotic, right?

I remember the emergency drills we had at school during the Cuban Missile Crisis when I was in kindergarten and first grade. An alarm would sound, and everyone would immediately crawl under their desks. Worry and fear invaded my mind: "Were the Cubans coming to get us?" I remember thinking, "If we get bombed this desk will fall on my head."

My anxiety followed me into adulthood and skyrocketed when I became a parent. How would I keep my children safe in a harsh and violent world? How would I keep them healthy (especially during the season when we were living in Sudan as missionaries)? What were the best parenting methods to raise kids to love Jesus and want to follow Him? My questions were endless and my fears varied.

In college, I discovered the joy of the book of Psalms. I began each day reading some, writing them out, and borrowing the words in my prayers. It felt like the psalmists were giving voice to many of my feelings. I discovered that they didn't give easy answers for negative emotions. Instead, they invited me to feel all my emotions and bring them to God. As I copied their words in my journal, as well as my own thoughts and feelings, my heart found comfort. I felt understood. It was as if the psalmists were my empathetic friends.

While still in the journey of raising kids, I was diagnosed with breast cancer. Nothing sends anxiety into a tailspin quite like cancer! Questions flooded my mind: Would I be alive to finish raising my kids? Would I live to see them married and having children of their own? How would cancer impact their faith? I dove into Psalm 46 and Psalm 27, memorizing both. God needed to become my refuge in a new, relevant, and life-sustaining way!

As I grappled with the severity of my diagnosis, a mentor of mine challenged me to begin each day by praising God. At the time it felt ridiculous. Who feels like praising God for cancer? Right? Yet, I figured I had nothing to lose. In addition to memorizing the Psalms, I began borrowing the words of the psalmists to praise God. "God, I praise You! You are my refuge and strength! You are my ever-present help in times of trouble. Even with cancer, I will not fear. You are with me and I praise You" (based on Psalm 46:1, 5).

The more I studied the Psalms, the more I discovered that the psalmists practiced a two-step rhythm: They poured out their hearts to God authentically and then praised God by faith passionately.

When they poured out their hearts, their honesty was raw. They held nothing back and didn't worry about how their anger, hurt, or worry was coming across to God. They just dumped! "Strike all my enemies on the jaw!" (Ps. 3:7). "How long, LORD? Will you forget me forever?" (Ps. 13:1). Wow! Don't you feel like praying that sometimes? Their praise was equally exuberant and passionate. "Let them praise his name with dancing and make music to him with timbrel and harp" (Ps. 149:3). Imagine uninhibited and unreserved dancing-in-the-aisles, throw-your-hands-up-and-shout type of praise.

As I began to practice this two-step process, **pouring out my heart, and then praising God by faith,** I felt a shift in my spirit. Gradually, faith replaced fear, peace replaced worry, and joy replaced anxiety. New confidence and courage rose, not in myself, but in God's goodness and what He could do through me. You see, friend, "God invites us to bring before Him our rage, doubt, and terror—but He intends for us to do so as a part of worship."[1]

WHAT ABOUT YOU?

I wonder about you. Have any worries? Fears? Anxiety? Concerns? Anything keeping you up at night?

> *"They poured out their hearts to God authentically, and then praised God by faith passionately."*

I'm guessing you do, and research backs my assumption. Anxiety disorders are the most common and pervasive mental disorders in the United States. In fact, an estimated 264 million people worldwide have an anxiety disorder. Women are nearly twice as likely as men to be diagnosed with an anxiety disorder in their lifetime.[2] The COVID–19 pandemic skyrocketed anxiety, fear, and depression. While you might not have a diagnosable anxiety disorder, you may still have some worries or be dealing with residual fear after the pandemic. Perhaps you're just stressed and overwhelmed. Let's face it, in our fast-paced, packed-full lives, there are quite a few things to feel anxious about.

Is God angry with us for our anxiety? No. As the psalmist writes in Psalm 103: 13–14, God is a compassionate Father who is aware that we are dust. We are human. Does He want to help us live victoriously over our anxiety? Yes. Does He want us to experience joy? Yes. How do I know? Because it's written all throughout His Word.

Our key verse for this study is "**When anxiety was great within me, your consolation brought me joy**" **(Ps. 94:19).** The idea behind this verse is when our anxieties multiply—and they do, don't they?—it's God's comfort that calms us down and settles us in joy. That's the extraordinary power of praise! As you praise Him in the middle of your anxiety, the Holy Spirit awakens your soul to His presence and the Holy One calms you down. Why don't you take a moment and write out that verse on a card, and then tape it to your mirror? It would be a great idea to memorize those words.

DIG IN, DIVE DEEP!

As you begin this study, I encourage you to dig in and dive deep. The Psalms, a collection of poetic masterpieces, are worship songs written mostly by King David. A few others were written by Moses and Asaph. The word "psalm," or *mizmor* in Hebrew, means "an instrumental song, a song accompanied by musical instruments."[3] The Psalms were basically the Jewish hymnal for worship in the tabernacle. As people would walk up the stairs to the temple they would sing the Psalms of Ascent. As they gathered, their psalms of praise filled the sanctuary.

God has called His people to worship (Ex. 34:14; Matt. 4:10; John 4:24). Why? Is God some insecure, egotistical being who needs continual affirmation and a daily "Attaboy"? No. God created us to worship Him because we become like what or who we worship (Ps. 115:8). As you worship God, the Holy Spirit strengthens your faith and you gradually become more like Christ.

This is why worship is key to overcoming anxiety. Each psalm is filled with emotion and written authentically, expressing genuine worship. As we spend time worshiping God, He transforms us. Gradually we find courage and joy replacing fear and anxiety. The Psalms are the perfect place to start your worship journey because the psalmists are always authentic.

At times the psalmists' worship is jubilant and filled with joy; other times it's filled with lamenting and weeping. The psalmists describe exuberant, dancing worship; at other times, they show us how to bow down in reverence and worship. The vast expressions of emotions and postures make the Psalms powerful tools for you to use in your own private worship journey. The language is raw, honest, engaging, and beautiful. After a while, the psalmists will seem like close friends, and you'll be comforted realizing they wrestled with all the same feelings you've experienced.

As you study the background of each psalm, you'll begin to understand that praise isn't just some glib hallelujah when life's going well. Praise is your intentional offering of worship, strengthening your faith and unlocking the key to joy no matter your life circumstances. It is absolutely the most effective path out of anxiety that I know.

Before we go any further, I want to invite you to pause a moment and honestly answer five key questions. These are personal questions. No one is going to check your answers. They are just between you and God, and there's not a wrong answer. They are designed to help you consider where you want to go with this study.

A FEW QUESTIONS TO CONSIDER

Consider these five questions before you begin. Feel free to journal your answers.

1. How much space is worry, fear, or anxiety taking up in your mind?
2. If your life were worry free, how would it look different?
3. How do you want to show up at work, at school, or in your relationships?
4. How does worry take away from how you want to show up?
5. How is worry or anxiety helping you?

WHAT YOU CAN EXPECT FROM THIS STUDY

As you begin this journey and dive into the Psalms, I want you to know I'm for you. The Psalms are absolutely one of my favorite portions of Scripture.

Praise is your intentional offering of worship, strengthening your faith and unlocking the key to joy no matter your life circumstances.

I feel so understood when I read them, and I'm hoping you do as well.

Each week we'll study several psalms. Open your Bible! Keep a pen and highlighter nearby. As you read these psalms circle key phrases, underline key thoughts, or write a date in the margin of your Bible to remember how God used the psalm in your life. (Always feel free to mark up your Bible.) We'll examine each one and consider what the psalm teaches us about overcoming worry through worship. We'll study the background of each and draw out practical applications for our lives.

Each week includes five days of homework. I know. Your life is crammed full, and the last thing I want to do is add more anxiety over tasks you need to finish. But let me assure you, the homework is only to help you reflect on the psalm and determine what is going on in your heart. So, make it work for you. Don't stress if you can't finish a day. Just praise God that you got some of it done and catch up later if that works for you.

An average day's homework will take about twenty minutes. Not bad, right? Each day will include the following sections:

A Morning Prayer—I am a firm believer in praying Scripture. So each day will begin with a short prayer based on a passage from a psalm to help you get your heart focused on God.

Explore—This section will include a guided study of a psalm. Again, open your Bible. You'll have the opportunity to peruse other Scriptures related to the psalm and to answer a few questions relative to the day's topic. You'll explore and study key words related to worship, and these words will give you a deeper understanding of the concepts being taught.

Selah—Pause and Reflect—Through the book of Psalms you will notice the word *Selah*. This means pause and reflect. This section includes some reflective questions to help you apply what you're learning from the Psalms. I would encourage you to take your time with these questions. There are no right or wrong answers; they're simply designed to help you understand what's in your heart and how you might surrender more of your anxiety to the Lord through worship.

Memorize—Each week you'll have one or two verses from a psalm to memorize. Committing verses to memory allows you to access those verses more quickly in your prayers and in the event of an unplanned anxiety attack. The Holy Spirit will use the Scriptures you've memorized to calm your heart.

Listen—One of the key tools God has used to quiet my anxiety has been worship music. I believe this might help you as well. Every day there will be one or two contemporary worship songs suggested. If you take the time to listen to the songs and allow them to prompt your praise, you will begin to experience God's presence more deeply. There in His presence, anxiety and fear are calmed.

Evening Praise—Each day ends with a short prayer of praise based on a psalm. Again, as you praise God, the Holy Spirit will calm your anxious heart.

Additionally, at the end of the study, you will find a listening guide that goes with the six-week video teaching that is available for this series.

Are you ready to begin? I'm excited for you to get started because I think you are just going to love the Psalms. I want you to know that I am praying for you and believing that this study is going to be life-changing for you. The freedom and joy you will experience as you learn to worship and let go of anxiety will radically transform you! If it does not, contact me at becky@beckyharling.com and I'll pray for you!

Blessings and Calm,

Becky

WEEK 1

FACING YOUR FEARS

WHEN I FEEL FEAR RISING, HOW DO I VIEW GOD?

MORNING PRAYER

Lord, You know my anxious thoughts.

This morning, I claim the words of

the psalmist, David:

You, LORD, are my light and my salvation.

Whom shall I fear?

Today, let me walk in courage

and with a sense of calm.

BASED ON PSALM 27:1

As I write this, we are living in some very wonky days! The recent COVID-19 pandemic has turned our world upside-down. Many have lost their lives, their jobs, and their security, as scientists scramble to develop a vaccine. At the same time, racial injustice, riots, and political polarization have filled the news and social media feeds. Horrific hurricanes and fire storms have raged over our planet and left many shaken to the core.

In 2016, *Time* magazine featured an article claiming that Americans are more afraid than ever.[1] Consider, that report came out long before 2020, a year that the world will never forget. Fear is a global problem, not just an American phenomenon.

The world in which the psalmists lived, though less sophisticated, was just as evil and dangerous. David had to flee for his life and hide in the wilderness for many years. Though anointed by the prophet Samuel to be the next king of Israel, David spent many years hiding from Saul, the current king, who gave orders to have David killed (1 Sam. 19:1). Imagine, a death threat! That would stir up a bit of fear, right?

This week we'll be looking at four different psalms that address the anxiety of perceived danger and fear. Today we begin with Psalm 27.

EXPLORE

READ PSALM 27 OUT LOUD

Often the Psalms will start out with the psalmist pouring out his heart to the Lord with requests. In Psalm 27, David leads right off with praise. He pours out his heart in the middle of the psalm (vv. 4–12), and then at the end he comes back to praise (vv. 13–14).

READ PSALM 27:1

David writes, "The LORD is my light and my salvation—whom shall I fear? The LORD is the stronghold of my life—of whom shall I be afraid?"

David uses three word pictures to describe God in this first verse. List the three word pictures below. Next to each one, write a sentence describing what that word picture teaches you about God.

READ PSALM 27:2-3

Bible scholars feel David is rehearsing past experiences in these verses where he saw the Lord protect and deliver him. It is highly possible that he is reflecting on his experience of fighting Goliath.

READ 1 SAMUEL 17:26-50

Where did David's confidence come from when facing Goliath? How did this victory over Goliath impact David's faith and prepare him for future battles with fear?

READ PSALM 27:4-12

When I walked through breast cancer almost twenty years ago, anxiety and fear were constant companions. During that season I remember memorizing Psalm 27. It has become one of my favorites whenever I feel fear rising. **How many times in these verses does David reference the presence of God?**

Circle the phrase "One thing" in your Bible. David could have asked for many other good gifts: protection, provision, courage, or good health. Instead, he set his focus on only one thing, God's presence. How might an undivided heart diminish fear?

At the time David wrote this, "the House of the LORD" would have been the tabernacle where the Jewish people went to worship. In the New Testament, Paul writes that our bodies are now the place where the Spirit of God dwells.

David cried out for the Lord to hear his heart and to answer his request. What was his request?

I love the New Living Translation of Psalm 27:8. It reads, "My heart has heard you say, 'Come and talk with me.' And my heart responds, 'LORD, I am coming.'"

David viewed his relationship with God as intensely personal. He heard God's voice, perhaps not audibly, but with ears of faith in his spirit. The Lord delights in us coming to talk with Him as well. He never tires of hearing His children cry out to Him. While we often cry out to Him in times of danger, He longs to carry on a continual conversation with us like a loving father with a child.

Many have experienced abandonment from their mother, father, or in some cases both. Broken homes are often the norm. As adults the wounds we experienced in childhood can leave us wrestling with an undercurrent of anxiety. **What does this verse teach about God's ability to heal deep wounds from childhood?**

READ PSALM 27:13–14

At the end of his psalm, David comes back to the heart of worship, writing: "Yet, I am confident that I will see the LORD's goodness" (NLT). A worshipful heart cries out, "God is good even though life feels scary."

Courage is not the absence of fear.
It is taking the next step by faith,
trusting that God is good
and that He will work all things
together for our good.

BASED ON ROMANS 8:28

SELAH—PAUSE AND REFLECT

What part does remembering God's faithfulness in the past play in building your courage for the future?

How might using word pictures to describe God's protection enhance your worship experience?

If you were to assign one word picture to God that best describes how safe you feel with Him, what would that word picture be?

As we look this week at the fears that create anxiety within us, what are some of the fears you wrestle with?

How might seeking the presence of God help quiet those fears?

Finish this statement based on today's lesson: When I feel fear rising I will . . .

MEMORIZE: Psalm 27:1

LISTEN: "Nothing Else" sung by Cody Carnes

POUR OUT YOUR HEART

In the space below, pour out your heart to the Lord and ask Him for strength and courage as you face fear.

EVENING PRAISE

Lord Jesus, as I close out this day
I remain confident of Your goodness.
As I sleep, I praise You that I can remain confident
and rest secure in Your presence and power.

BASED ON PSALM 27:13, 3

WHEN YOU NEED A SHELTER

MORNING PRAYER

Lord, as I begin this new day

I lift my eyes to You.

When fear and anxiety assail,

I will keep my eyes on You.

Only You can release me from the trap of fear.

BASED ON PSALM 121:1; 25:15

I'll never forget the phone call from the doctor that informed me I had breast cancer and that the safest method of treatment for me was a double mastectomy. Nothing really shakes the foundation of your core quite like the word "cancer." It becomes a haunting invisible enemy. Fear pummeled my mind in new ways. I was still in the thick of raising kids and I wondered, would I live to finish raising them?

During that season I memorized Psalm 46. Every day before my surgery, I took a long walk and recited the words of the psalmist, "God is my refuge and strength, an ever-present help in trouble, therefore we will not fear…" (Ps. 46:1–2). The words of Psalm 46 allowed my imagination to form pictures of God being a refuge to me, a place to pull back and hide in the chaos of all the doctor appointments and decisions I needed to make. God's presence became so real to me during those dark days. I still often return to Psalm 46 when fear threatens to overwhelm me.

EXPLORE

READ PSALM 46 OUT LOUD

What word pictures does the psalmist give that depict the presence of God?

READ PSALM 46:4–5

Natural disasters seem to abound—earthquakes, hurricanes, fire storms, raging waters, and floods. In these verses, the writer paints a picture, in contrast to the chaos depicted by natural disasters, of a peaceful river. **What do you think the peaceful river represents?**

READ PSALM 46:6–7

In what way do these verses remind you of the political environment we face today?

Even though nations are divided and polarized, what is the comfort found in verse 7?

READ PSALM 46:8-9

When the psalmist writes about "desolations," he is referring to terrifying events that leave us astonished. In His sovereignty, God allows horrific events. We don't always understand why, but we do know that He promises to use even horror for good in the life of one who believes and trusts Him (Rom. 8:28). God will ultimately allow terrifying events to abolish evil. How do you think God might use catastrophic events to change the hearts of people?

READ PSALM 46:10

This is one of the most quoted verses in the Psalms. When fear terrorizes and chaos abounds, our minds are anything but still. Yet God calls us to "be still" in His presence knowing that He will be exalted over all things. **Stillness refers to a quiet trusting. It does not refer to silent worship. How might worshiping and praising God bring our hearts to a place of quiet trust?**

SELAH—PAUSE AND REFLECT

READ PSALM 46:11

The psalmist closes his song by painting a picture once again of God as a fortress. A fortress is a place built to protect. In this day where it seems the enemy of our souls is on a rampage, what does it look like for you to shelter down in God's protecting fortress?

As you reflect on Psalm 46, which verse speaks to your own personal situation the most?

What does it mean to you personally that God is an ever-present help?

How might praising God help you understand more fully that God is your refuge and fortress?

MEMORIZE: Psalm 27:1

LISTEN: "Be Still" sung by Red Rocks Worship, Acoustic Sessions

POUR OUT YOUR HEART

Write out a prayer expressing your desire for God's presence to calm your fears.

EVENING PRAISE

I praise You, Lord God,

that You are my refuge and strength.

Thank You that You are an ever-present help in times of trouble.

I praise You as I end my day, that You will quiet my heart

and help me to rest securely in You.

I leave every worry and fear at Your feet,

knowing that You alone are my fortress.

BASED ON PSALMS 46:1, 2; 4:8; 52:22

WEEK 1 | DAY 3

SHOULD I FEEL GUILTY THAT I WRESTLE WITH FEAR?

Fear is one of the strongest tactics that Satan, our enemy, uses against God's people. While we are not to give Satan our focus, we are to be wise in understanding his antics (1 Peter 5:8). In Revelation 12:10, John writes that Satan is "the accuser of our brothers and sisters" and that he "accuses them before our God day and night."

Wow. What a job description. All Satan can do is accuse us and lie (Rev. 12:8). He takes truth and twists it to terrorize God's people and provoke them to fear.

His entire existence is wrapped up in trying to deceive people and get them to doubt God's goodness.

For example, imagine for a moment you feel fear in the middle of the night. Then you start feeling guilty for feeling fearful. You begin beating yourself up thinking, "I should trust God more. What's wrong with me?" Next thing you know you can't fall back to sleep, because now you're in a tailspin feeling not only fear, but guilt for your fear. Or maybe your kids are out driving, and it's past the hour they were to be home. Your mind starts imagining, "What if they were in a car accident? What if they're stuck in a ditch?" Your what ifs continue until, before you know it, you have your children dead and buried.

Satan uses your guilt to shame you and make you feel terrible about yourself. He also pummels your imagination with every fear and possibility he can throw at you. Soon you are living through nightmares you were never intended to live through. **The key is not to feel guilty for fear but to know the weapons that are available and use them to fight back!**

Today we're going to look at Psalm 91 and a few related passages to discover some of the weapons we can use when Satan starts with his nonsense.

EXPLORE

READ PSALM 91 OUT LOUD

In the very first verse, the psalmist uses the word Almighty to describe God. The word Almighty in the Hebrew is *shadday*. Often it appears as *El Shadday* in the Old Testament and means "God Almighty." It speaks to the mighty and unconquerable nature of God.[2] God is all-sufficient and all-powerful to meet any foe that comes against His children. He is all-powerful over Satan and all his shenanigans. God's sovereign power trumps every other. He is eternally able to protect His children.

In your Bible, circle the word "dwells." The key to quieting fear and anxiety is to dwell in God's presence. What is the outcome the psalmist points to for those who abide in the presence of God?

In these first two verses, the three distinct names for God are used: *Elyon* (the most high God),[3] *Shaddai*, (the Almighty), and *Elohim* (the supreme God).[4]

What do these names of God speak about His ability to protect and care for you and your loved ones?

What are the two word pictures the psalmist creates for us in verse 2?

READ PSALM 91:3–9

Fowlers were bird catchers before the days of guns. They used nets spread on the ground and various traps to capture all kinds of birds. The fowlers provided birds to the marketplace for sacrifice and food.[5] When David writes, "Surely he will save you from the fowler's snare," he is comparing the crafty fowlers to the crafty tactics of the evil one to trap and ensnare you. What types of snares or traps do people fall into when they are afraid?

Pestilence refers to attacks that come in the form of plagues. Often the enemy will use fears of sickness and illness to torment moms. Immediately following this reference, we see the "motherly" nurturing side of God. The picture of God covering us with His feathers reminds us of a mother hen spreading her wings out to protect her baby chicks.

READ PSALM 91:9

What is the condition to not being overwhelmed by fear?

READ PSALM 91:14–16

Even though the child of God is not promised a life free from sorrow or suffering, what is promised here?

SELAH—PAUSE AND REFLECT

What images did you grow up with about God?

How does Psalm 91 paint a different picture?

When you imagine God covering you with His wings, how does that make you feel?

Friend, the next time you feel guilty for feeling fear, shift your focus. Rather than beating yourself up because you're not braver or stronger, start worshiping your God who is bigger, stronger, and more amazing than any enemy you face.

MEMORIZE: Psalm 27:1

LISTEN: "Psalm 91 (On Eagles' Wings)" sung by Shane & Shane

POUR OUT YOUR HEART

Take a portion of Psalm 91 that especially resonates with you and write out a prayer based on those words.

EVENING PRAISE

Lord, I praise You that You are El Shadday,

the God who is Almighty.

Thank You that I don't have to live in bondage to fear.

I praise You that You are my refuge and that Your faithfulness

surrounds me as I sleep.

BASED ON PSALM 91:1, 9

TOOLS TO FIGHT BACK

MORNING PRAYER

Lord Jesus,

You are good and all that You do is good.

As I begin this new day, strengthen my faith to trust You more.

When fear or worry attack my mind today,

help me to remember that You are good!

BASED ON PSALM 119:68

When one of our daughters was in college in upstate New York, her car broke down on a country road. Bethany didn't have a cell phone and wasn't sure what to do. Mustering all her courage, she approached a house and knocked on the door. Thankfully, a kind woman invited her in, offered her tea, and called help for her. Bethany made it back to college safe and sound.

Later that night, I lay in bed in our home in California thinking about all the things that could have gone wrong. She could have been left stranded; she could have knocked on the door of a serial killer; she could have foolishly tried to walk miles back to campus in the cold. My mind went ballistic with worry and fear.

All of a sudden, I realized what I was doing, and I shifted my focus immediately. I needed to rein in my fear and **turn my panic into praise.**

I began praising and thanking God that my daughter was safe. I praised God that He loved Bethany more than I did, and He would protect her with or without me. I praised Him for being a God so caring that He would position a sweet older lady to invite Bethany in and offer her tea. Gradually, I fell asleep peacefully.

> *I needed to rein in my fear and **turn my panic into praise.***

Here's the truth: because fear and anxiety are such large tactics used by the enemy against us, we must come up with a battle plan! Here's a plan that you can use anywhere and at any time!

EXPLORE

TURN YOUR PANIC INTO PRAISE

READ PSALM 56 OUT LOUD

David had fled from King Saul, who was trying to kill him, into the land of the Philistines. However, some men spotted him there and went to the king in Gath, where David was hiding, to warn the king. David felt fearful of King Achish and, out of fear, acted insane so that he wouldn't be recognized as the great warrior David (1 Sam. 21:10–15). Many Bible scholars believe that it was in this context that David wrote Psalm 56. He begins by pouring out his heart to God.

READ PSALM 56:1-2

Describe the tone of David's prayer in the space below.

READ PSALM 56:3-4

I remember as a young mom teaching these verses to my kids when they were small. One time when we were on an airline flight, my two toddlers grabbed each other's hands and started saying out loud, "When I am afraid, I will put my trust in YOU!" I've got to admit, hearing them apply what I had taught them brought a lot of joy to my heart.

In your Bible, circle the words, "I put my trust in you." Then underline the phrase "In God, whose word I praise." What do you feel is the correlation between praising God and developing trust?

Do you think trust is an emotion or a choice? Why?

READ PSALM 56:5-8

David returns to pouring out his heart to God. He "vents" honestly before the Lord. List his complaints in the space below. What does David's honesty teach you about prayer?

READ PSALM 56:9–11

We, as humans created in God's image, have the ability step back from our thoughts and analyze them. This is what David does in verses 10–11. They echo verses 3–4. It is as if David is holding a self-management meeting. He reassures his heart and asks himself the question, "What can man do to me?"

You will often see this pattern through the Psalms where the psalmist considers his thoughts and then questions himself. What benefit do you see in holding a private self-management meeting when you feel fear overwhelming you?

READ PSALM 56:12–13

After analyzing his fears, David makes a very strategic choice in these verses. What is that choice?

SELAH—PAUSE AND REFLECT

I have heard it said that another way to view trusting God is to think of relaxing in God's goodness. I have personally found it helpful during particularly stressful seasons to remind myself, "Becky, relax in God's goodness."

When you think of relaxing in God's goodness what comes to mind?

What would it look like personally for you to relax in God? What spiritual practices could you put in place to help you relax?

MEMORIZE: Psalm 27:1

LISTEN: "Victory is Yours (Live)" by Bethel Music & Bethany Wohrle, Victory (Live)

POUR OUT YOUR HEART

In the space below write out a prayer to God expressing your battle with fear. Then use one of the verses you listed above to pray Scripture and take authority over your fear.

For example: *Father, You know how much I battle fear and worry when my kids are out driving [or list some other worry]. Lord, I don't want to worry, but I do. Lord Jesus, I praise You that You give me authority over my fear. You promise to be my refuge and strength when I am afraid. Thank You that You promise me that You will answer my kids when they call on You, and You will be with my kids when they drive, even in times of trouble. (Pss. 46:1; 91:15)*

EVENING PRAISE

Lord Jesus, I praise You for this day.

Thank You for Your protection throughout the day.

I confess to You, Lord,

sometimes my worries and fears come at me like angry wasps,

especially at night.

But I lay each one down at Your feet, and

I praise You that I have all authority in Jesus' name.

I exalt You, Lord Jesus, and I accept Your peace.

BASED ON PSALM 118:24, 12, 10

PRAISING THE NAME OF JESUS CHRIST

MORNING PRAYER

I praise You this morning, Lord Jesus.

I love You.

Thank You that today, when I face

fear, worry, or anxiety,

I can cry out to You.

You will listen and bend down to answer my prayers.

BASED ON PSALM 116:1–2

There are, according to most commentators, at least twenty-five different psalms that include a prophetic reference to Jesus Christ.[6] These Messianic prophecies are quoted in eleven different New Testament books. One of the most loved of all the Messianic Psalms is Psalm 110. It has been called "The Royal Psalm." It paints a prophetic picture of Jesus Christ as Messiah, King, and Priest.

It is quoted in the New Testament more times than any other psalm. Jesus Himself quoted this psalm with reference to the fact that He was the Christ, the Messiah (Matt. 22:43–45; Mark 12:35–37; Luke 20:42). Open your Bibles, and let's take a look at this prophetic masterpiece!

EXPLORE

READ PSALM 110 OUT LOUD

READ PSALM 110:1

In Psalm 110:1, there are two different names used for God. The first is the Hebrew *Yahweh*, and the second is the Hebrew *Adonai*. Yahweh carries the idea of "the One who brings something into existence."[7] Adonai means "Messiah."[8] In other words, David writes, "The Lord of the universe, the One who created all things, says to my Lord, the Messiah, sit at my right hand until I make your enemies a footstool for your feet."

To be a Messiah is to be a Savior. This is the way Jesus revealed Himself to the woman at the well. He introduced Himself as "the Messiah." (John 4:25–26). As the Messiah, Jesus came to break the curse of sin over our lives and to save us from the penalty of sin.

David prophetically gives us a glimpse into the loving relationship between God the Father and Jesus Christ the Son.

The word "says" that is used in verse 1 is a unique Old Testament word that is only used in prophetic verses.[9] In other words, this is a direct prophecy referring to the coming Messiah, Jesus Christ.

Not only is Jesus the Messiah, who can deliver us from fear of sin and the consequences of sin, but He is also the King. When the Father said to the Son, "Sit at my right hand," He gave Him all authority. He then went on to say, "Until I make your enemies a footstool for your feet." How does this verse demonstrate that, ultimately, all things will be placed under the authority of Jesus Christ?

Not only is Jesus the Messiah, He is King!

READ PSALM 110:2-3

The word "scepter" is a word that speaks to power and the Kingship of Jesus. The word "rule" speaks to the authority that Jesus Christ has. As you think about Jesus as King and having all power and all authority, how does that diminish fear?

There are moments in today's culture where I feel like we forget that Jesus is King. He rules over our lives, but He also rules and reigns over all world events. Nothing can happen without His permission. Does He allow evil? Yes, for a time. But He will ultimately be victorious over evil because He is the righteous King who will rule eternally.

When you feel afraid or confused, it's comforting to realize that the Messiah and King who has all power and authority is interceding for you before the Father!

Not only is Jesus the Messiah and the King, but He also is the Perfect Priest, who lives to intercede for us before the Father. Stop. Read that again. Did you catch it? When you feel afraid or confused, it's amazingly comforting to realize that the Messiah and King who has all power and authority is interceding for you before the Father! Friend, you have Jesus on *your* side! Incredible! Because He is on your side, victory is guaranteed!

READ PSALM 110:5-7

Jesus will eventually bring justice and right every wrong. It may feel as though evil is winning at times, and it may feel as though injustice rules the day. But Jesus will be victorious! He will crush those who come against Him. I don't know about you, but when I'm wrestling with anxiety and fear, I remind myself that Jesus will be victorious. Not only that, He promises if I am "in Him," I will be victorious as well!

SELAH—PAUSE AND REFLECT

Think about Jesus as Messiah, Your Savior; Priest, Your Advocate; and King, Your Ruler. Take each of those titles and write out a prayer of praise to Jesus, worshiping Him for that particular title.

Look up the following verses and write down the promise of victory that is given in each one:

Luke 10:19

John 16:33

1 Corinthians 15:57

Friend, Jesus is and will be victorious. And in Him, you have victory as well. Spend a few minutes focusing your praise on Jesus, the Victorious One.

How does praising Him as the mighty, victorious King quiet your fears and anxiety when the enemy comes against you with fear and worry?

The next time fear or anxiety pummel your thinking, claim the name of Jesus. When you spend time praising Him, the enemy will flee because Satan is allergic to praise.

Below you will find ten names or titles of Jesus. Next to each one, write a sentence saying how that name comforts and quiets your fear. Then spend a few minutes in prayer praising Jesus that He is each of the attributes listed below.

Almighty One—Revelation 1:8

Advocate—1 John 2:1

Bread of Life—John 6:35

Rescuer—1 Thessalonians 1:10

Good Shepherd—John 10:10–11

Great Sympathetic High Priest—Hebrews 4:14

Immanuel—Isaiah 7:14

King of kings—Revelation 19:16

Light of the world—John 8:12

Victorious One—Revelation 3:21

MEMORIZE: Write Psalm 27:1 from memory in the space below.

LISTEN: "Turn Your Eyes" by Natalie Grant / The Belonging Company

POUR OUT YOUR HEART

Write a prayer, first pouring out your heart about a struggle you have with fear. Then shift your focus to praise, and use three of the names for Jesus listed above to write out a prayer exalting Jesus Christ over your fear.

EVENING PRAISE

Lord Jesus, as I end this day,

I exalt You as the

King of kings and the Lord of all lords.

I praise You that You are my Messiah, my King, and my Priest.

Thank You that I can trust You.

I praise You that at Your name eventually every knee will bow.

BASED ON PSALM 110; PHILIPPIANS 2:10

ADDITIONAL NAMES AND TITLES OF JESUS CHRIST

Here are twenty-five additional names or titles of Jesus Christ. Use these in your private worship time to defeat the enemy and strengthen your faith. I have found this to be a great way to quiet anxiety.

Alpha and Omega, the Beginning and the End—Revelation 1:8

Pioneer and Perfecter (or Author and Finisher) of our faith—Hebrews 12:2

Beloved Son—Matthew 12:18

Counselor—Isaiah 9:6

The Creator—Colossians 1:17

Deliverer—Romans 11:26

Everlasting Father—Isaiah 9:6

God's Messiah—Luke 9:20

Great High Priest—Hebrews 4:14

Head of the Church—Ephesians 1:22

Holy One—Acts 3:14, Mark 1:24

Horn of Salvation—Luke 1:69

I Am—John 8:58

Jesus—Matthew 1:21

King of Kings—1 Timothy 6:15

Lamb—Revelation 13:8

Lord of All—Acts 10:36

Mediator—1 Timothy 2:5

Messiah—John 1:41

Mighty God—Isaiah 9:6

Morning Star—Revelation 22:16

Prince of Peace—Isaiah 9:6

The Life—John 14:6

The Way—John 14:6

The Truth—John 14:6

WAITING WHILE YOU WORSHIP

HOW LONG, LORD?

MORNING PRAYER

Lord Jesus, I confess, I am impatient.
I am longing for You to answer me in my waiting.
When I'm waiting, it's so easy for me to doubt Your goodness
and forget Your faithfulness.
Remind me, Lord, through my day
that You are sovereign and Your plans for me are good,
even when I can't see You moving.

BASED ON PSALM 13:1; JEREMIAH 29:11

Before COVID-19 shut everything down, I had been working with a trainer at the gym. I remember when she looked me in the eye and said, "Becky, you need to learn to be patient, girl!" Truer words have never been spoken! I like to see things happen fast and have had to battle a sense of hurry in almost every area of my life. My trainer went on to explain that the personal training takes a while before you see tangible results. It's similar in our spiritual journeys. God is never in a hurry, have you noticed? He generally takes much longer to answer our prayers than we would like.

Nothing stirs up anxiety quite like waiting. When we're waiting for a diagnosis, a job opportunity, an evaluation of our child, a financial turn-around, or an answered prayer, anxiety seems to skyrocket. Yet, waiting is a foundational spiritual discipline for the believer. Like physical training, it is spiritual strengthening for our souls.

Author Eugene Peterson wrote, "We wait for God to do what we cannot do for ourselves in the depths."[1] As we wait, our spirits press into God, and His Spirit strengthens our core spiritual muscles.

Pause and think for a moment. What have you been waiting for?

- Salvation of a loved one

- Direction for your future

- Healing for a relationship

- Repentance on the part of a prodigal

- Financial turn-around

- A child of your own through pregnancy or adoption

- A godly spouse

David, the writer of Psalm 13, understood the anxiety of waiting. Anointed by Samuel as King over Israel as a young man, David had to wait fifteen years for the fulfillment of his anointing. In the season of waiting, David wrote this psalm.

EXPLORE

READ PSALM 13 OUT LOUD

Listen to the anguish in David's soul. How would you describe David's feelings?

David poured out his heart to God, "How long, LORD? Will you forget me forever?" (Ps. 13:1). At the end of Psalm 13, David penned these profound words, "But I trust in your unfailing love; my heart rejoices in your salvation. I will sing the LORD's praise, for he has been good to me" (Ps. 13:5–6). What gave him the ability to write those words with such faith? I believe it was his choice to worship as he waited.

READ PSALM 13:1–2

In these verses, David is wrestling with his thoughts. He feels forgotten by the Lord and as though the Lord is hiding His face from him. In his waiting journey, David wrestled with thoughts of being abandoned by God. Theologically, David most likely understood that God would never abandon him, but he was wrestling with doubt.

In what ways does waiting tempt us to doubt God's goodness and provision in our lives?

David asks the Lord to look at him and listen to his cries. He asks the Lord to restore the "light to his eyes." What David means here is essentially, "put the sparkle back in my eye." In what way does this point to the despair David was feeling?

The "dark night of the soul" is a concept that many who are believers have experienced. The concept first came from a poem written by St. John of the Cross. John of the Cross (1542–1591) was a reformer. He was a Catholic priest who is known for his deep spiritual writings. He, along with St. Teresa of Avila, was the founder of the Discalced Carmelites. The dark night of the soul referred to a sort of spiritual depression that God often allows believers to journey through. It is often through the journey of the dark night of the soul that the Holy Spirit begins to work into the believer's life a poverty of human spirit where, emptied of all else, Christ becomes all.

What evidence do you have from Psalm 13 that supports the idea that David was experiencing a dark night of the soul?

Write out Psalm 13:5–6 in the space below. Circle the word "trust."

Trust is tricky for many of us. We want to trust God's goodness even when we're waiting, but sometimes we just can't get our emotions to cooperate. How would you personally define trust? What do you think gave David the confidence to rest in God's unfailing love?

David ends his psalm with a choice. What is his choice as recorded in Psalm 13:6?

SELAH—PAUSE AND REFLECT

Think of an area of your life where you are waiting. Write about that situation.

At times when we're waiting, we are triggered to doubt and tempted to despair. What action can you take to build up your trust in God's unfailing love while you wait?

How does this psalm demonstrate the rhythm of pouring out your heart and then praising God?

MEMORIZE: Psalm 13:5–6

LISTEN: "Take Courage" sung by Kristene DiMarco

POUR OUT YOUR HEART

In the space provided write a prayer to the Lord about how you feel when you are waiting.

EVENING PRAISE

Lord, I praise You that You are the Alpha and Omega.

You hold time and eternity in Your Almighty hands.

Thank You, that even when I don't see You working,

I can trust that You are working all the circumstances

of my life together for my good.

I worship You that as Sovereign God,

nothing and no one can thwart Your plans.

I praise You that Your timing is perfect!

BASED ON REVELATION 1:8; PHILIPPIANS 4:13; JOB 42:2

WHAT'S GOD DOING WHILE WE WAIT?

MORNING PRAYER

Hear my cry, O God;

listen to my prayer.

Father, I long to see Your will come in my life

and in the lives of those I love.

Holy One, as I wait for You to answer my prayers

shape my heart toward Yours.

Refine me so that I can be used by You to greater effect.

As I wait, I bow before You,

and my heart cries, "Holy."

Your ways are always right and Your timing always perfect.

You are my strength;

I will watch for You as I wait.

BASED ON PSALMS 61:1; 59:9

When we are in a season of waiting, it's easy to get frustrated. As we mentioned yesterday, we are tempted to believe that God has forgotten us or that He's simply aloof to our requests. What if, instead, God had a far greater purpose in our waiting?

What if, as we waited, we praised Him in advance of the answer He would give? I believe our spiritual lives would be strengthened.

As we search the Scriptures, we find that God uses delay in our lives for at least two purposes: **To polish us as His instruments, and to set the stage for His will.**

EXPLORE

Today we're going to consider several psalms that explore the concept of waiting.

1. Delay polishes us as His instruments.

V. Raymond Edman, former president of Wheaton College, wrote, "Delay never thwarts God's purpose, rather it polishes His instruments."[2] I have often gone back to this quote, as I am an impatient person. Dr. Edman reminds me that God's goal in my life is not to keep me happy but to transform me into His image. That being the case, He will often use the discipline of waiting to refine and shape my character.

READ PSALM 66:10–12

Here the psalmist writes that God "refined us like silver" (v. 10). Why do you think it's important for Christians to be refined?

David also had to be refined in order to be the leader God had called him to be. Author Bob Sorge writes about David: "The years of delay, from the time of promise to the time when he actually became king, were used as a refining fire by God to purify David and prepare him for the throne"[3] From a simple shepherd boy to mighty king was quite the leap. David needed time to mature, wait in God's presence, learn to listen more carefully to God's voice, and grow in deeper dependency on God. How gracious that the Holy One forced David to wait. Otherwise, David would never have been able to handle the challenges he would face as king and he might never know the deep intimacy that was forged in the presence of God as he waited.

The psalmist writes, "But you brought us to a place of abundance" (v. 12). How do you think waiting produces abundance in our lives?

2. Delay positions the stage for God's will.

There are times when your waiting might not have as much to do with you personally as it does with what God is trying to accomplish around the world. God has all the seasons measured. He knows the appointed time when He can best accomplish His will (Ps. 75:2). This was certainly part of God's plan in Joseph's life.

READ PSALM 105:16–22

Remember Joseph? When he was just a young boy, God gave Joseph the dream that he would someday become a great leader. However, because Joseph was the eleventh child in a family of twelve, the idea sounded not only preposterous to his family but also arrogant. On top of his crazy dreams, Joseph was Daddy's favorite. His brothers had enough of the trophy, dreamer child, and they had Joseph sold into slavery. I'm sure there were many times when Joseph wondered if the dream God put on his heart was just a farce. But, at just the right moment in history, God used Joseph's influence and power to save his father and family who eventually became the nation of Israel.

READ PSALM 105:24

What was the blessing of Joseph's long wait?

How does this echo the words of Psalm 66:12?

SELAH—PAUSE AND REFLECT

Almost anyone who has ever been used by God has gone through a time of waiting on the Lord. It is a key spiritual discipline. We see this in Hudson Taylor's life.

Hudson Taylor, a hero in the world of missions, returned home from serving as a missionary in China due to illness. His illness rendered him laid up for five years. Hudson must have wondered if God was finished using him. But, while Hudson waited to get well, God was polishing His instrument and positioning the world stage for the greatest work of Hudson's life. It was during his period of waiting on God when God gave Hudson the vision of China Inland Mission. When reflecting on the long dark years of waiting, Hudson wrote, "Without those hidden years, with all their growth and testing, how could the vision and enthusiasm of youth have been matured for the leadership that was to be."[4]

Has there been a time in your life when God has refined you by allowing you to go through a season of waiting?

What were some of the lessons you learned during that season?

From your perspective, how does waiting strengthen a heart of worship and praise in us?

MEMORIZE: Psalm 13:5–6

LISTEN: "Here I Bow" by Jenn Johnson

POUR OUT YOUR HEART

Write out a prayer to God in the space below expressing your heart as you wait.

EVENING PRAISE

Lord, even though it is uncomfortable for me,

I praise You for the seasons of waiting that You've

allowed in my life.

Thank You for the precious moments and hours spent on my knees
before You.

I praise You that though You have refined me through waiting,

You have brought me seasons of abundance.

Thank You that when I cry out to You

You bend down to listen.

I praise you Lord,

that You have heard my cries.

You have not rejected my prayers or withheld Your love from me.

BASED ON PSALM 66:10-12, 19-20; 116:2

THE POSTURES OF WAITING WITH HOPE

MORNING PRAYER

In the morning, Lord, You hear my voice;

in the morning, I lay all my requests before You

and wait expectantly,

believing that You will answer in Your grace and goodness.

Help me today to wait with

expectant hope for the answers You will bring.

As I wait let my heart sink down deeply into You,

trusting that You are good and Your plans for me are good.

I bow down before You today.

BASED ON PSALM 5:37

Today and tomorrow, we're going to study Psalm 37 and consider the postures of waiting in worship with hope. This is one of my favorites! There's so much in this power-packed psalm that we need to divide it between two days. Before we dive into the text, let me give you a little background.

This psalm is an acrostic psalm. For the most part, each pair of lines begins with a successive letter of the Hebrew alphabet. For centuries worshipers have learned to use whatever alphabet they have as a prompt to praise God. Praising your way through the alphabet is an easy spiritual practice. You simply find a character trait of God that begins with each successive letter. David, the writer of this psalm, was amazing at this and many of the psalms are alphabetical poetic masterpieces!

David wrote this while in a season of waiting himself. Isn't it good to know that others have had to learn to wait on God as well? David gives us five postures of worship that help us wait with hope.

EXPLORE

READ PSALM 37 OUT LOUD

POSTURE 1: Kneel in trust rather than pace with worry (Ps. 37:1–3)

David dives right in, and you have to wonder if he was instructing his own soul as well as ours: "Don't fret." When we're waiting, our minds can at times go ballistic! We spin off a million "what if" scenarios and soon we're completely anxious. Often our anxiety leads to anger. Our hearts argue with God, "Why don't you step in and do *something?*"

READ PSALM 37:1 AGAIN

According to this verse, what contributes to our worry and anxiety?

We have control over our minds. This is why the apostle Paul instructed us to "take every thought captive" (2 Cor. 10:5). As human beings created in the image of God, we have the capacity to step back from our worry and to direct our thoughts. Rather than directing your thoughts toward all the "what ifs," take charge of your mind and direct your thoughts to the character of God. This is the basis for our trust.

As human beings created in the image of God, we have the capacity to step back from our worry and to direct our thoughts.

What do you think it means to "trust God"? How would you describe trust to a friend? Is it a feeling or a choice?

When we bow in trust we say, "God, You are good. Your ways are good and Your every intention toward me is good. I bow and surrender to Your goodness in this situation that I have no control over. I trust—declare it out loud—Your goodness and grace to carry me!" Andrew Murray is one of my favorite authors. He wrote, "The lower we bow, the nearer God will come and make our hearts bold to trust him."[5]

Since worry and anxiety have been such a battle for me, I've had to learn to figure out a plan to take charge of my mind. So, here's my plan:

> When worry spins my mind into a frenzy
> over things I can't control,
> I get on my knees and open my hands.
> I take control of my mind
> and direct my thoughts toward the goodness of God.

POSTURE 2: Raise your hands in praise rather than distracting yourself with cheap substitutes (Ps. 37:4)

WRITE OUT PSALM 37:4

The word for "delight" in the Hebrew means to be soft or pliable.[6] In English the word means to take joy in something. You need a soft heart to find your joy in the Lord. Waiting triggers in us frustration with the Lord. From there we may begin to doubt—"Is God really good? Does He really have my best interests in mind? Maybe He has forgotten me?" In those moments, rather than moving closer to the Lord, we move away from Him and try to find consolation in other delights.

David suggests that rather than running to cheap substitutes, you praise God, and in so doing, you make your hearts soft toward His will. The more you praise and delight in God's character, the softer your heart will become toward Him. I know that it can feel counterintuitive, but I promise you, as you praise Him by faith, your feelings will follow.

What is the promise for those who praise that's found in Psalm 37:4?

The Hebrew word for "heart" that's used in this verse alludes to "the intellect, awareness, mind, inner feelings, and deepest thoughts."[7] How does the Holy Spirit influence our innermost desires when we praise and worship Christ?

POSTURE 3: Roll your burden over to God rather than doing the heavy lifting (Ps. 37:5)

The word that's used here for "commit" is the Hebrew word meaning "roll."[8] The word gives us a great visual. I go to a gym to work out and do some weight training. But some weights are way too heavy for me. Rather than picking them up, I can find the strength to roll them. The same holds true in the spiritual strength training of waiting. You can't lift the burden. It's too heavy. But the Holy Spirit gives you the strength to roll it onto the Lord and commit to leaving the burden in His Almighty hands.

READ PSALM 37:6

What is the promise for those who commit their burdens to the Lord?

SELAH—PAUSE AND REFLECT

Think through the three postures of waiting that we've talked about today. Which posture is the most difficult for you and why?

How is waiting with hope an act of worship?

What do you feel like God is saying to you about waiting with an attitude of hope?

MEMORIZE: Write out Psalm 13:5–6 in the space below.

LISTEN: "I Will Wait for You" (Psalm 130) by Shane & Shane

POUR OUT YOUR HEART

In the space below, pour out your heart to God about a situation in which you are waiting.

EVENING PRAISE

Lord, I praise You that as I wait and take delight in You

You will make my steps firm.

I praise You that I can trust You with _____

[Name a circumstance where you are having to wait].

I praise You that as I wait

You are developing strength in my life.

I roll my burdens on to You,

trusting that You will work even as I rest.

BASED ON PSALM 37:23; 37:5

THE POSTURES OF WAITING IN WORSHIP WITH HOPE

MORNING PRAYER

Let nothing disturb me today, Lord.

Let nothing frighten me today.

All the pressing issues of my life will eventually pass away.

God, You are unchangeable.

Patience gains everything.

She who clings to God will lack nothing.

God alone is sufficient.

Teach me to trust as I wait, Lord.

BASED ON THE PRAYER OF TERESA OF AVILA[9]

Today we're going to continue looking at the postures of praise for waiting well. Each posture demonstrates a bowing of our will to our most Holy Sovereign God.

EXPLORE

POSTURE 4: Sit still rather than taking action (Ps. 37:7)

Write out Psalm 37:7 in the space below. Circle the word "patiently."

I've gotta be honest with you. Being still is *so* incredibly hard for me. When God isn't moving fast enough, in my human nature, it's easy to think, "Why, I'll just help Him out!" Here's the thing: God doesn't need my help or yours.

- He doesn't need you to nag your husband to read his Bible and go to church with you.

- He doesn't need you to pester your adult kids, buying them books that you feel will lead them back to Christ.

- He doesn't need you to "fix" your coworker or anyone else for that matter.

- He doesn't need you to rush ahead of His plan and try to manipulate circumstances in your favor.

- He needs you to sit and wait in prayer.

READ 2 SAMUEL 7:1-5, 12-13

After David had finally become king and was all settled in the palace, he wanted to design and build the temple of the Lord. David had such a heart for worship, it seems reasonable that he would long to construct a place where people could come and worship. He verbalized his desire to Nathan the prophet, and it made sense to Nathan. So the prophet told David, go ahead and do it! Basically, Nathan was saying, "Wow! What a great idea! I'm sure the Lord would be behind a project like that." But then Nathan heard the voice of the Lord.

What was the Lord's answer to David's desire?

READ 2 SAMUEL 7:18

After hearing the Lord's answer, what did David do?

David's choice to set aside his plans in favor of the Lord's shows us a posture of absolute surrender. It is so hard for many of us to sit still in the presence of the Lord. Author Eugene Peterson wrote, "David sat. This may be the single most critical act that David ever did, the action that put him out of action—more critical than killing Goliath."[10]

Why do you think God often calls us to "be still" when everything in us wants to take action?

How do you think waiting for the throne helped David to trust the Lord when God told him no about building the temple?

When we wait patiently for the Lord in stillness, we stop wrestling and worrying. Our souls are quiet. Andrew Murray described it this way, "Having our thoughts and wishes, our fears and hopes hushed into calm and quiet in that great peace of God which passes all understanding."[11]

Often as mothers, grandmothers, or aunts, we have hushed the cries of an infant. As the infant is gently rocked to sleep snuggled close in our arms, they are quieted and rest peacefully in our arms. This is the picture of how God Almighty wants to hush our fears and worries as we wait. He snuggles us close, inviting us to rest secure in His timing. The peace we experience in His presence goes far beyond our human understanding.

POSTURE 5: Bow your will rather than shake your fist (Ps. 37:8)

When we bow our will, we surrender to Almighty God, trusting that He is working even when we don't see it.

One of the most difficult times to bow our will and wait for God is when we're being criticized. We long for Him to step in and straighten out our critics! In those seasons, we long for God to right the wrong done to us, but even then God calls us to be patient. He invites us to trust Him with justice and for us to simply wait for God to vindicate us. While we wait, He performs a deep work in our hearts, bringing forth the fruit of meekness.

READ PSALM 37:11

What is the correlation between waiting and meekness?

What is the promise for those who are meek?

Meekness is not weakness. It is strength under fire and it is what Jesus modeled for us.

SELAH—PAUSE AND REFLECT

In what situation are you tempted to take matters into your own hands rather than waiting for God?

READ PHILIPPIANS 2:5-8

How did Jesus demonstrate meekness for us? What can you learn from Jesus in the realm of humility?

READ PSALM 37:34

What does hope look like tangibly for you as you wait?

MEMORIZE: Psalm 13:5–6

LISTEN: "Refiner" featuring Chandler Moore and Steffany Gretzinger, Maverick City Music / TRIBL Music

POUR OUT YOUR HEART

Write a prayer to the Lord describing how you feel about waiting for Him to vindicate you when you've been wrongly accused.

EVENING PRAISE

Lord Jesus, I praise You that You are my stronghold

in times of trouble.

I thank You that while I am still,

You are not.

You are working.

I praise You that You will fight my battles as I remain silent.

Lord, as I rest,

I praise You that I can take refuge in You.

I trust You with every situation.

I praise You that Your plans are good, perfect, and holy.

BASED ON PSALM 37:39-40; EXODUS 14:14; JEREMIAH 29:11

WAITING IN HIS PRESENCE FOR REVIVAL

MORNING PRAYER

Lord, I praise You for a new morning.

I remember seasons when You showed great favor to me.

Holy One, revive me again.

Let a passion for Your presence overwhelm my soul.

Restore me, O God;

make Your face shine upon me today.

I will listen for Your voice today,

thanking You for Your promise of peace.

Bring revival as I call on Your name

and wait in Your presence.

BASED ON PSALM 85:4, 8; 80:7, 18–19

I've been reading about the Hebridean Revival that took place in the tiny village of Barvas, Scotland, between 1949–1953. The revival began with two elderly sisters. One was eighty-two and crippled with arthritis, and the other was eighty-four but completely blind. One night as they sat by the fire, they began to feel burdened for the little church across the field from them that had no young people. While they realized they couldn't go out and recruit young people, they knew they could pray. As they began to pray, one of the sisters had a vision of young people filling the church. The following morning the sisters asked the local pastor to their house and told him that he needed to get ready because a revival was coming. Pretty bold, don't you think?

The minister asked what he should do. The women gasped as they repeated, "What should you do? You should pray, man!" They proposed a deal to the minister and told him if he would gather his people twice a week to pray in the barn at one end of the village, they in turn would pray from their house from ten at night until three in the morning.[12]

Late night prayer meetings began, and at one point, one man stood and read Psalm 24. He asked the people to confess their sins and make sure their hands and hearts were pure. He reminded the people of the village that they needed to wait in the presence of the Lord for revival. The presence of God filled the barn. Some fell on their faces before the holiness of God and revival came to the Hebrides.[13]

A preacher named Duncan Campbell came to the small village and night after night preached the gospel. One of the first meetings lasted till four in the morning. Duncan Campbell led countless people in the village to the Lord. Duncan defined revival as "a community saturated with God."[14]

Here's what struck me about this story. First of all, it was two elderly crippled ladies that persisted in prayer for revival and felt sure they had heard from God that it was coming. Secondly, people gathered, prayed, and waited in the presence of the Lord for revival to come. You see, friend, without a willingness to press into prayer and wait in the Lord's presence, revival likely won't happen. If our communities are going to be saturated with the presence and power of God, we need a renewed commitment to persisting in prayer, waiting in worship, and seeking His face.

The story of the Hebridean Revival compels me to want to spend more time on my knees, waiting in God's presence, worshiping Him, and crying out for Him to bring revival. This is what Asaph—the writer of Psalm 80—did.

EXPLORE

READ PSALM 80 OUT LOUD

READ PSALM 80 AGAIN SILENTLY

Circle every instance of the words "restore" or "revive." In your own words, write your own definition of "revival."

READ PSALM 80:5

How might difficulties and trials lead us into a place of revival?

READ PSALM 80:8–11

These verses are a reference to when God used Moses to lead His people out of captivity in Egypt and established Jacob's descendants as Israel. The "vine" here is Israel. Out of that vine will come "the Vine"—Jesus Christ (John 15:1–8).

READ PSALM 80:14–17

In these verses, we find a strong prophetic reference to the coming Messiah out of the vine of Israel. In verse 16 the psalmist writes, "Your vine is cut down." In what way was the Messiah "cut down"?

READ PSALM 80:17

The psalmist writes, "the son of man you have raised up for yourself." What is this a reference to?

READ PSALM 80:18–19

The psalmist ends by crying out for God to revive and restore the people of God. What part does waiting play in pursuing God in prayer for revival?

SELAH—PAUSE AND REFLECT

A part of every revival is a dying to self and a resurrection to the new life we have in Christ. Often, we forget that the call to follow Christ and receive His life is a call to follow His example and die. Without something dying, it cannot be revived.

Read the following passages. Consider what each one says to you personally. Then write your thoughts next to each one.

John 12:24

Galatians 2:20

Colossians 3:1–5

MEMORIZE: Write out Psalm 13:5–6 from memory.

LISTEN: Listen to "God of Revival" (featuring Brian Johnson & Jenn Johnson). As you listen, make it your personal prayer for revival.

POUR OUT YOUR HEART

Write out Psalm 80:18–19 in your own words as a prayer and plea for revival. Remember, revival starts with you.

EVENING PRAISE

Father, I praise You that just as You led the people of Israel

out of captivity,

You can lead me into the freedom

of a deeper relationship with You.

You guided them safely, so that they were unafraid.

As I cry out to You for revival,

thank You that I don't need to be afraid;

You will lead me.

Lord, I praise You that Your heart is for

revival, not only for me but also for my city.

Come, awaken me.

Awaken my city, my nation, and nations around the world

to the power and presence of the resurrected Christ.

I praise You that Your will is that people

from every nation, tribe, and tongue will stand before

the throne, worshiping You.

BASED ON PSALM 80:8; 77:53; 79:10; REVELATION 7:9

LAMENTING WITH AUTHENTICITY

WHEN YOUR WORSHIP IS WEEPING

MORNING PRAYER

Lord Jesus, lover of my soul,

I praise You that You are

a Savior well acquainted with grief and sorrow.

Thank You that You see my tears

and You actually keep track of them.

I praise You that You never shame me for crying.

Instead You comfort me with Your Holy Spirit.

Let me live in authentic worship today,

not denying my feelings but laying them on the altar before You.

BASED ON ISAIAH 53:3; PSALM 56:8

Years ago, I had a light blue couch. I loved that couch. It was where I knelt each morning and poured out my heart to the Lord. Often in my times of deep worship, I wept. After a while I began to affectionately call it my "weeping couch." It was a treasured place where I poured out my heart to the Lord. Gradually, on one of the cushions, a stain developed.

After one of my surgeries for cancer, I lay in my bed resting when my teenage daughter came into the room and said, "Mom, you better hang on to the bed! Dad's selling everything!" Then she went on to say that Steve had sold my weeping couch. I groaned but didn't have the energy to take action. We were getting ready to move across the country, and Steve knew I wasn't physically up for packing, so he did what made sense at the time.

Ah, my weeping couch was gone! He sold the couch to a couple who was convinced they could get the stain out. Steve figured I wouldn't want it because of the stain. It took me a little bit, but I did forgive him! However, I never forgot that weeping couch because it represented so many hours on my knees before the Lord.

Weeping has an honored place in the life of the believer. When David was captured by the Philistines, he wrote about his tears: "You keep track of all my sorrows. You have collected all my tears in your bottle. You have recorded each one in your book." (Ps. 56:8 NLT). Jesus Himself was a man of sorrows and well acquainted with grief (Isa. 53:3). In John 11, at the tomb of Lazarus, He wept even though He knew He would raise Lazarus from the dead a few minutes later.

I don't believe that God ever intended that our praise and worship journey was to be all "happy, clappy." Sure, there will be times of great celebration, but often in our journey there will be sorrow, broken relationships, and difficult challenges. For those times in our lives, the psalms of lament touch our souls in a way that others can't.

At least one-third of the Psalms are laments. What exactly is a lament? A lament is a prayer to God, where we vocalize our protests and ask two important questions: "Where are you, God?" and "Why did you allow this?" In the words of author Dan Allender, "The laments of the Psalms encourage us to risk the danger of speaking boldly and personally to the Lord of the universe."[1]

When we lament

we pour out our sorrows,

our anger, our frustrations,

our doubts, and our fears.

EXPLORE

READ PSALM 55 OUT LOUD

Write down your first impressions.

In this psalm, David felt betrayed by a close friend and wept before the Lord. His emotions were raw as he begged God to listen to his prayer. In his weeping, David cried out for God's presence to come close and for an escape from the pressure.

READ PSALM 55:1–8

What expressions does David use as he laments before the Lord?
List them in the space below:

In these verses, David gets to the issue that has triggered his lament. What is that issue?

Betrayal is one of the hardest issues to deal with. It's often easier to forgive an enemy than a friend who betrays us. When friends are disloyal, we feel our trust has been violated and our soul has been torn.

Jesus knew this feeling. He Himself was betrayed in the garden. Judas betrayed Him with a kiss (Matt. 26:49). Peter denied even knowing Him (Matt. 26:69–75). Though Jesus was fully God, He was fully human and as such the betrayal He felt must have been brutal.

How does knowing that Jesus Himself was betrayed encourage you to be honest with Him in your prayers when you've been betrayed?

READ PSALM 55:22

In his prayer, David encourages himself, reminding himself to cast his cares on the Lord. What is the promise contained in this verse for those who cast their burdens on the Lord?

The Hebrew word for "sustain" that is used in this verse means "to maintain, nourish, provide food, bear, hold up, protect, support, defend; to supply the means necessary for living."[2] God nourishes the heart that has been betrayed and promises to be life support to those who cast their cares on Him. But the only way to cast those cares on the Lord is to pour out our hearts before Him.

READ PSALM 55:23

How does this verse reflect a heart of worship?

SELAH—PAUSE AND REFLECT

Some of us grew up with messages that made us think we couldn't feel or experience negative emotions. Here's the thing: we follow Jesus, who experienced every emotion just as we have, and He did so without shame or embarrassment.

READ ISAIAH 53:3

How does the prophet Isaiah describe Jesus in this passage?

READ MARK 14:18–20

How did Jesus experience betrayal? How does knowing that Jesus Himself experienced betrayal help you authentically deal with your negative emotions when betrayed?

MEMORIZE: Psalm 3:3

LISTEN: "The Story I'll Tell" performed by Naomi Raine, Maverick City Music

POUR OUT YOUR HEART

In the space below, pour out your heart to the Lord about a time when you felt betrayed. Dare to be honest.

EVENING PRAISE

Lord Jesus, I praise You that I can cast all my cares on You.
You have promised to nourish me as I cling to You.
I worship You because You rescue me from the battle unharmed.
Holy One, I bow before You.
You are the One who is enthroned above, and
yet You bend down to listen to my prayers.
Thank You in advance for how You will redeem for good
this situation in my life.
I trust You, Lord.

BASED ON PSALM 55:22, 18, 19, 23

WEEK 3 | DAY 2

WHAT DO I DO WITH MY ANGER?

MORNING PRAYER

Lord, may I use my mouth today to praise and extol You;

stand by me today, helping me to authentically admit

when I'm angry

to save me from mishandling my anger.

Often my heart is wounded when I feel betrayed by others.

Out of Your goodness and love,

deliver me from

cursing or condemning others.

BASED PSALM 109:30, 31, 21, 22

I felt angry! The constant criticism coming from those who didn't agree with the direction we were taking the ministry was wearing me down. It was still early in the evening, but I turned to my husband Steve and said, "Nothing good is going to come out of my mouth, so I'm putting my mouth to bed." Without another word I went to my room, crawled in my bed, and opened a book to read until I fell asleep. Ever felt that way?

Anger is one of the most confusing emotions that we experience. As believers in Jesus, we find ourselves conflicted, and anxiety rises to the forefront of our thinking. Is it right to feel angry? If I'm a good Christian shouldn't I always feel peaceful? If I do feel angry, should I deny it and pray it away? After all, Jesus said we are to love God and love others. How can I love those who I feel deep anger toward? What about those who I might consider to be my enemy? Jesus said we are to love our enemies (Matt. 5:44). How in the world are we supposed to do that authentically, admitting the truth about how we feel while still loving others? Those are some of the questions we'll explore this week.

Conflicts create stress and anxiety and cause a lot of pain in our lives. Author Peter Scazzero writes, "Conflicts offer us revelation and the possibility of reconciliation, but they can also leave us limping."[3] I mean who wants to be criticized or threatened? Yet conflict is a part of our broken world.

What I love about the psalms is that the psalmists are authentic about their anger! In fact, more than half the Psalms are psalms of lament in which the writer often complains to God about their anger over broken relationships.

EXPLORE

READ PSALM 3

This psalm was written by David when he was fleeing from Absalom, his son who had stirred up a rebellion against his own father. Absalom was not just trying to gain the throne, but he was looking to murder his father. Talk about betrayal!

You might wonder, "Does God allow that?" Oh, yes, He does because often we have to travel the difficult road of lament before we can reach the heart of true worship. Author Michael Card writes, "Lament is not a path to worship, but the path of worship."[4]

Write a couple of sentences describing what happened in this story.

How would it feel to have your son leading a rebellion against you?

READ PSALM 3 AGAIN

How would you describe the tone of Psalm 3?

READ PSALM 3:1–2

Circle the word "many."

The fact that David used this term several times in the psalm points to the traumatic feelings David was experiencing. The rebellion against David was growing. David felt threatened and angry.

READ PSALM 3:3–4

What adjectives would you use to describe David's attitude here?

Circle the word "shield" in verse 3.

A shield was often used as a symbol of God's protection. David cries out for God's protection. Interestingly, he doesn't just cry out for protection of his body. He prays for protection of his mind, "But you, LORD, are a shield around me, my glory, the One who lifts my head high."

READ PSALM 3:5–6

Anger is most commonly a secondary emotion. What do you think David's primary emotion was in Psalm 3?

In these verses we see David's full-blown anger. How does David express his anger to God?

David prays, "Strike all my enemies on the jaw; break the teeth of the wicked." That's a pretty bold prayer. I have studied this verse backwards and forwards. There have been times when, admittedly, I have prayed, "Lord, sock 'em in the mouth!" Have you ever wanted to pray something similar when someone has betrayed you, abused you, spread rumors about you, or hurt you in another way?

As I've studied this psalm, it seems David is picturing his enemies as a snake or wild beast with sharp fangs. That's a vivid picture, huh? Satan is pictured as a snake. He is the accuser (Rev. 12:10). He lives to criticize the people of God, day and night. Sometimes Satan even uses good people to accomplish his purposes. Consider this, we are never more like Satan than when we are tearing down another person.

Rather than joining with what God was trying to accomplish through David, Absalom started a revolt. David pours out his heart in prayer to the Lord and asks the Lord to strike his enemies on the jaw. Was he hoping God would punch Absalom in the mouth? Maybe. But he was also expressing, "Lord, render my son's accusations useless. Deprive him and those who have joined him of their ability to do evil."

In many Christian circles there is a pseudo-spiritualism that is governed by the rule, "Don't be angry. Deny your feelings and be calm all the time." Friend, that's not godly. That thought process is actually more Buddhist in thought. Jesus said

He was the truth (John 14:6). Denial is a lie. Jesus wants you to pour out your heart authentically and stop lying in your prayers.

Author Peter Scazzero writes, "Anger is a central discipleship issue for every believer. It is a signal alerting us to many potential messages from God—a warning indicator light on life's dashboard, inviting us to stop and pay attention to what God might be saying."[5] When something needs maintenance in my car, I receive a signal from the dashboard. If I ignore the signal or deny that it's there, my car develops a serious problem. The same holds true in our Christian walk. Feelings of anger alert us to the need that some part of our soul needs care.

> *Denial is a lie. Jesus wants you to pour out your heart authentically and stop lying in your prayers.*

As a loving and compassionate Father, God invites us to "get it all out," dumping our feelings at His feet. There He can heal us of our pain and help us to move forward toward forgiveness. This was exactly how God handled David. While David has his meltdown in the throne room, God doesn't wag His finger and scold, "Godly Christians don't get angry!" He doesn't shame him saying, "Pull yourself together, David, and act like a man!" He understands that David needs to get all his feelings out before he can get to the place of forgiveness. Ah, what a loving, compassionate God we worship.

After David has fully lamented, he worships God as being the only One who brings deliverance. His worship is passionate and genuine.

READ PSALM 3:8

How does this verse reflect a heart of praise?

SELAH—PAUSE AND REFLECT

What were the messages about anger you received while growing up?

Do you think anger and praise are compatible? Why or why not?

When you feel angry, what do you most often do (i.e., ignore it, deny it, explode in rage, or some other response)?

Spend a few moments asking God to examine your heart this week to help you grow in handling your anger in an emotionally healthy and spiritually healthy manner.

When you hear the word "anger," you might feel anxious. I encourage you to ask the Holy Spirit to open your heart and protect your mind as we begin.

MEMORIZE: Psalm 3:3

LISTEN: "Whatever Your Plan Is" performed by Josie Buchanan / Bethel Moment

POUR OUT YOUR HEART

Take a few minutes and ask the Lord to meet you specifically as we look at anger this week. Think about some of what you've experienced this past week. Is there any criticism or other circumstances that have stirred up anger in you? Spend time pouring out your heart to the Lord, honestly expressing what you feel. Use phrases in your prayer like "I feel."

EVENING PRAISE

Lord, from You comes deliverance.

I praise You that I can trust You with those who seek to hurt me.

I praise You that no matter what I feel, You are with me.

My anger does not separate me from You.

Search my heart, O God.

Show me if there is any offensive way that I need to confess.

I place all my feelings in Your Almighty hand.

May I rest unfrazzled and unworried, knowing I can trust You.

BASED ON PSALMS 3:8; 139:23–24

WHAT DOES THE REST OF SCRIPTURE SAY ABOUT ANGER?

MORNING PRAYER

Good morning, Lord.

I invite You to probe deeply into my life.

Test me and see if I've been honest with You or

if I've been living in denial.

Rescue me from faulty thinking.

Rise up, Lord.

Show me, Lord, where I need to embrace new thinking about anger.

Speak to me, I pray.

BASED ON PSALMS 139:23; 7:6

Today we're going to look at anger more specifically and consider how our anger might motivate us toward a deeper heart of worship and praise. I want to caution you before we begin—you're going to need to stop denying your anger today and look honestly at the anger looming beneath the surface of your life. It could be messy and complicated, so why don't you take a moment to breathe, and pray?

EXPLORE

READ PSALM 89:20-26

In these verses, God expresses both His protection of David and His anger toward David's enemies. How does God express His anger?

READ PSALM 89:14

Righteousness and justice are two core character traits of God, along with love and faithfulness. Sometimes in our Western culture we have dumbed down God's justice because we prefer to think of God as just a loving Father.

How is God's justice and righteousness part of God's anger?

Consider the following passages and write down what each one says about God being angry.

Deuteronomy 9:8

Exodus 32:10–11

Matthew 21:12–13

Clearly Scripture teaches that God gets angry and acts on His wrath. Now let me ask you another question. Are you made in His image? If you are, what is the implication about anger?

READ GENESIS 1:26-27

Part of your humanity as being made in the image of God is that you are able to feel and express your feelings like God. Just as God felt anger, you will as well, because you are made in His image. God calls us to be honest about our anger but also gives us some helpful boundaries.

Look up the following passages and write down the boundary contained in each verse.

Proverbs 29:11

Ephesians 4:26

1 Corinthians 13:1

READ COLOSSIANS 3:8

This verse is not saying that the emotion of anger is wrong. But it can become sin when we keep all our anger inside. We must get rid of anger by flushing it out by lamenting praise.

SELAH—PAUSE AND REFLECT

How might anger be a signal to let you know something needs attention?

What damage might be done to your soul if you deny your anger?

As you studied these verses, what did God speak to you?

MEMORIZE: Psalm 3:3

LISTEN: "Your Nature" sung by Kari Jobe

POUR OUT YOUR HEART

Write a prayer to the Lord pouring out your heart about anger. What has God spoken to you today and how will you respond?

EVENING PRAISE

Lord, I praise You that You have the ability to
transform my anger into something beautiful.
I praise You that You allow me the grace to
dump all my anger in the throne room.
I lay my enemies and those who have betrayed me at Your feet.
I praise You that I can trust You with justice.
I praise You that as I authentically release my anger,
Your Holy Spirit will help me in my weakness
and empower me to forgive.
May my forgiveness be a sweet offering of praise to You!

BASED ON PSALM 77:10; ROMANS 3:24; HEBREWS 4:15; ROMANS 8:26-27

WHAT ABOUT THE IMPRECATORY PSALMS?

MORNING PRAYER

Lord Jesus, I praise You that You have created me in Your image

with the ability to feel many feelings.

Help me today to walk in integrity,

not denying my feelings

but yielding my feelings to You.

I pray that when I feel sad or angry today

You will help me to process those feelings in healthy ways.

Help me to pray with complete honesty today,

yielding every feeling to You.

BASED ON GENESIS 1:26

I remember reading Psalm 109 for one of the first times and thinking, "Holy moly are we allowed to pray that way?" Well, hang on to your hats because this psalm that we're going to study today is going to blow your socks off, and you're going to wonder, "How did that get into the Bible?"

Psalm 109 is an imprecatory psalm. I think you're going to discover today that we can be completely honest with God—with all of our feelings, even the negative ones!

EXPLORE

READ PSALM 109 OUT LOUD

Wow! Right?! David was angry and hurt. Some scholars believe this psalm was written as the result of the many coups that threatened his reign as king. David basically unravels in the throne room and throws a royal fit! Consider some of the requests of David concerning his enemies:

"Appoint someone evil to oppose my enemy;
let an accuser stand at his right hand.
When he is tried, let him be found guilty,
and may his prayers condemn him.
May his days be few;
may another take his place of leadership.
May his children be fatherless
and his wife be a widow.
May his children be wandering beggars;
may they be driven from their ruined homes.
May a creditor seize all he has;
may strangers plunder the fruits of his labor.
May no one extend kindness to him
or take pity on his fatherless children."

PSALM 109:6–12

Psalm 109 is called an imprecatory psalm. The imprecatory psalms are psalms of lament that call down judgment or curses on enemies.

The questions on your mind are probably: How in the world did that psalm make it into the Bible? Is this to be a pattern for my prayers? How does this fit with Jesus' call to forgive? I mean Jesus is the one who calls us to "love your enemies" (Matt. 5:44).

David's prayer doesn't seem very loving, does it? Yet it demonstrates raw authenticity before God.

When we read David's psalm, we are given an authentic picture of raw feelings of anger. David is disappointed with God and angry at his enemy. Anger is a real emotion, and God does not want us to deny our anger. If we're going to truly love our enemies, we must first admit that we have enemies and that we are angry. Denial is simply lying to ourselves. God is a God of truth (John 14:6). He calls us to authenticity. Author Michael Card writes:

> We are a people in perpetual denial of the hidden hate we have for our enemies . . . Jesus showed us that hatred is a wound that must be healed, that denial is a paralysis only He can heal.[6]

Friend, the truth is our wounds must be drained of the poison of hate before we are able to forgive.

READ PSALM 109:21–22, 30–31

What do these verses teach us about the need for us to be completely honest before God?

After David completely melts down before God, exhausted and drained, he cries, "But you, Sovereign LORD, help me for your name's sake; out of the goodness of your love, deliver me. For I am poor and needy, and my heart is wounded within me" (vv. 21–22). He ends with a triumphant cry of praise, "With my mouth, I will greatly extol the LORD; in the great throng of worshipers I will praise him. For he stands at the right hand of the needy, to save their lives from those who would condemn them" (vv. 30–31). There at the altar of worship, David lays down his hatred, delivering his enemies into the hand of God and trusting Him with justice.

Forgiveness is often a process

that leads us through the dark valley of lament,

where we release the poison in our souls,

but ultimately leads us to the altar of worship.

What we know to be true of David is that when Saul finally dies, committing suicide, David weeps without bitterness in his soul (2 Sam. 1:19–27). When his son Absalom dies, the enemy who tried to take his throne, David weeps like a heartbroken father without a trace of bitterness (2 Sam. 18:29–33).

SELAH—PAUSE AND REFLECT

READ PSALM 109

Do you think it's right to pray imprecatory prayers? Why or why not?

How is forgiveness an act of worship?

Do you think forgiveness is a one-time decision or more of an ongoing process? Why?

MEMORIZE: Psalm 3:3

LISTEN: "Defender" performed by Rita Springer

POUR OUT YOUR HEART

Write out a prayer to God expressing your feelings about a relationship in which you are struggling to forgive. Pour out your anger and leave it at the feet of the Almighty.

EVENING PRAISE

Oh Father, I praise You that I can boldly enter Your throne room
and be completely honest.
You allow me to express both my rage and sadness,
inviting me to pour out my heart like water before You.
As loving Father, You hold me close as I dump it all out.
I praise You that as I leave all those feelings
at Your feet
You will empower me to do the impossible,
which is to forgive.
I praise You that I can trust You with justice and vengeance.
I leave all my feelings in Your hands tonight.
Help me to rest free and at peace.

BASED ON HEBREWS 4:16; LAMENTATIONS 2:19; PSALM 4:8

WHAT ABOUT WHEN YOU'RE WRONG?

MORNING PRAYER

Lord Jesus, thank You that Your mercies

are new every morning!

Each day I try to keep my heart aligned with You

but, O Lord, so often I fail.

I make faulty assumptions about others,

I often fall into patterns of judging and criticizing others.

Father, as I enter this new day,

I ask You for the grace to see my own faults,

and for continued mercy as I repent and move forward.

Keep my heart tuned to You today.

BASED ON LAMENTATIONS 3:22–23; PSALMS 51:1; 125:4

When our relationships with people are broken, it often is a reflection of a broken relationship with God. This was true for David.

In the spring, when the kings usually went to war, David stayed home in his cushy palace and sent Joab instead. One evening, David went out to walk on his roof where he had quite the view. Below in the valley was a beautiful woman bathing. David could have walked back inside and left well enough alone. Instead, he sent a messenger to find out who the beautiful woman was and brought her to the palace where he had sex with her.

A little while later, she became pregnant and sent word to David that she was pregnant with his child. It was obvious that it was not her husband's baby as he was away in battle. David tried to cover his sin by giving Bathsheba's husband, Uriah, leave so he could sleep with his wife. But Uriah was a man of integrity, and it bothered him that he would be given special privileges while his friends were out fighting. David then had his general put Uriah on the front lines so he would be killed. Then David took Bathsheba into his home and made her his wife. You can read the whole story in 2 Samuel 11:1–27. The last words of 2 Samuel 11 are haunting: "But the thing David had done displeased the LORD" (2 Sam. 11:27b).

Later, Nathan the prophet came and confronted David. David could have become defensive or shifted the blame. Instead, he felt the conviction of the Holy Spirit and wrote a lament over his sin. Turn to Psalm 51 in your Bible, and let's explore the passage together and see what we can discover about the role of confession in our lamenting.

EXPLORE

READ PSALM 51 OUT LOUD

How would you describe David's attitude in this psalm?

Often, when we've wronged another, it's easy for us to become angry and we see the other person as being completely at fault. Rarely is that the case. Most often if you have a broken relationship, part of the fault is yours. In those moments it's time to borrow the penitent words from Psalm 51 so that you can experience forgiveness from God and from others.

READ PSALM 51:2-5

Circle the word "sin" in your Bible.

In our culture today, "sin" is not a friendly word. Calling it out can be perceived as judgmental or prudish. And when we wrong others, it's easy to try to "save face" by offering excuses or shifting the blame elsewhere. David doesn't blame Bathsheba; he doesn't blame his tiredness or boredom. He simply calls his wrongdoing sin.

What is sin?

> Sin is anything that breaks our relationships
>
> with God or others.

We are commanded to love God and love others. Whenever we act unkindly, talk behind someone's back, take advantage of another, put another down, or fail to love someone with our whole heart, we have sinned.

The good news is that we have Jesus, who is our atoning sacrifice and advocate before the Father. This means we don't have to feel afraid to confess our sin. We can come before God with nothing to hide, bow in His presence, confess our brokenness, and turn from our patterns of sin. This is exactly what David did.

READ PSALM 51:1-5

Write down some of the phrases David uses as he confesses and repents of his sin.

Sometimes when people lament over their sin, they are really grieving that they got caught. That is not repentance. What evidence do you have from Psalm 51 that David truly repented and turned from his sin?

READ PSALM 51:7

Hyssop is a plant grown in the Middle East that was used to sprinkle blood as part of the Jewish Passover.[7] David is crying out for God to take a hyssop plant and sprinkle blood over him to forgive and cleanse his sinfulness. God required a blood sacrifice for the forgiveness of sins (Heb. 9:22). Now, friend, because of Jesus' shed blood on the cross, every sin you have committed or will commit is covered by His grace. We repent to restore us to a right relationship with God.

READ PSALM 51:8–15

What are some of the requests that David makes in this section?

READ PSALM 51:17

How is a broken and contrite spirit a form of worship?

SELAH—PAUSE AND REFLECT

Is it easy or hard for you to admit when you're wrong?

When was the last time you felt true sorrow over your sin?

Is there anyone to whom you owe an apology? What action steps do you need to take?

MEMORIZE: Psalm 3:3

LISTEN: "O Come to the Altar" by Elevation Worship

POUR OUT YOUR HEART

David prayed, "Restore to me the joy of your salvation, and grant me a willing spirit, to sustain me" (Ps. 51:12). Take that prayer and write out your own version in the space below.

EVENING PRAISE

Lord, I praise You that You are a grace-giving and merciful God.

Thank You that You are a compassionate Father

who is slow to anger but who abounds in love.

I praise You that You don't keep a record of all my wrongs.

Reveal to me the thought patterns that lead me down a path to sin.

Remind me that as I take every thought captive,

You will guard my thoughts from unhealthy patterns.

I praise You that with You there is always forgiveness

and acceptance.

BASED ON PSALM 103:13, 8; PSALM 130:3, 4; 2 CORINTHIANS 10:5

PRAISING GOD LEADS
TO CONTENTMENT

WEEK 4 | DAY 1

WHAT'S MISSING?

MORNING PRAYER

Lord Jesus, You have called me to live a life of contentment.
I confess, I often fall short.
Oh Holy One, how often I compare myself to others,
longing to have their gifts, their looks, or their possessions.
As I begin this new day,
remind me that Your love is better than life.
Help me to worship You and find
deep contentment there in Your presence.

BASED ON 1 TIMOTHY 6:6; PSALM 63:3

Social media is all sorts of fun, isn't it? I love connecting with friends and family on Facebook and Instagram. The other day I was in line, waiting and scrolling on my phone through Instagram. All of a sudden, my stomach grew a bit anxious as I realized other friends of mine were doing an awesome job keeping up with creating posts while I was obviously lagging behind. And their posts were good! That's when it hit me. What was I doing? Comparing myself to others! Never. A. Good. Idea.

Ever been there? Maybe for you it's not keeping up with the expectations of other professionals. Maybe it's comparing yourself to the young mom on Instagram who just gave birth and is back in her size 2 skinny jeans in six weeks. Later, as a result, you feel frustrated and inadequate. Or maybe it's seeing on Facebook the roses your friend's husband gave her for Valentine's Day, when yours needed the reminder that it was even a holiday. So you end up feeling hurt and a bit angry with your husband. Maybe after browsing a magazine you look around your house and perceive inadequacies in your decorating skills and your budget.

Comparison stirs up envy, leaves us feeling anxious, and robs us of the contentment that God wants us to experience. Yet it's so very human. All of us have longings, and when those desires aren't met and we see another person thriving, the temptation is to compare. The psalmist Asaph described it so well, "But as for me, my feet had almost slipped; I had nearly lost my foothold. For I envied the arrogant when I saw the prosperity of the wicked" (Ps. 73:2–3). Whether or not the person is wicked is not really the point of where we're headed. The point is, if you want to be a contented person, you need to stop comparing.

David also understood the temptation to compare and wrote several beautiful psalms teaching us that the key to contentment is learning to praise God. This week, we're going to study three different psalms. The first is perhaps the most familiar. Open your Bible to Psalm 23.

EXPLORE

READ PSALM 23 OUT LOUD

READ PSALM 23:1

David begins with a rather startling statement: "The LORD is my shepherd, I lack nothing." Did you catch that? Nothing!

Read that statement over several times and circle it in your Bible. It's startling, right?

Let's break it into two statements:

The Lord is my Shepherd. The word for Lord that's used here is the Hebrew word *Yahweh*.[1] It was the most popular name for God used by the children of Israel. Yahweh is the all-sufficient, self-sustaining creator of the entire universe—and of you.

Roi is the Hebrew word for "shepherd,"[2] and it means the God who provides loving care. If you think about the fact that God is completely self-sustaining and the only one capable of providing for our every need and loving enough to do so, it's staggering. Based on this absolute assurance in God as his shepherd, David then goes on to write:

I lack nothing. Nada. Zilch. Not. A. Thing.

As you look at your life, what things come to mind that are lacking right now?

What do you think is the key to being able to say wholeheartedly with David, "I lack nothing"?

As you think about those two statements, write a statement describing God's character in your own words. Then imagine what life would look like for you if you lacked nothing. Write a statement about what that would be like.

Honestly, we could sit with this one verse all day. What if we repeated it all day, focused our attention on it, meditated on it, and digested it?

READ PSALM 23:2-3

David makes four promises about how the Lord takes care of His sheep. What are those four provisions? List them in the space below:

How do the four promises help you personally with finding contentment?

How do you think praising God helps you understand His leading in your life?

READ PSALM 23:4

David wrote, "Even though I walk through the darkest valley, I will fear no evil." Write your own "even though" statement in the space below. Here's an example: Even though I walk through cancer, I will fear no evil.

David goes on to write, "For you are with me." Friend, the key to walking through dark valleys without fear is the presence of God. David writes two tools that the shepherd used to comfort his sheep. What are the two tools mentioned in Psalm 23:4?

I like to think of **the rod** as representing the Word of God and **the staff** representing the Holy Spirit. When you learn to combine using Scripture and unleashing the power of the Holy Spirit through praise, you will have far greater victory over anxiety and in the end enjoy more contentment.

Circle the word "comfort."

The Hebrew word for comfort that is used here is *nacham*, meaning "to comfort, console, extend compassion, sigh with someone who is grieving."[3] In other words, we have a Shepherd who empathizes with us in our sorrow.

READ PSALM 23:5

The psalmist writes that the Shepherd anoints his head with oil. Like the prophet Isaiah, David understood that the Shepherd would anoint his life with the oil of joy (Isa. 61:1). Oil was often scented with perfume or certain spices to give people a lift in their spirits and a sensation of pleasantness.[4] Throughout Scripture, oil is also used as a symbol or a metaphor of the Holy Spirit (Isa. 61:1).

Here's what you need to know: the Shepherd, God Himself, wants *you* to experience joy and gladness. One of the greatest ways to access that is to spend time praising Him. As you praise Jesus Christ, the Holy Spirit unleashes joy in your soul that is unlike other fleeting waves of joy. If you don't believe me, try it. Consistently praise God for seven days and see if you don't experience more joy and contentment.

READ PSALM 23:6

David ends the psalm with a type of personal blessing. It's as if he is praying these words over himself. But they are also for you! "Surely goodness and love will follow me all the days of my life, and I will dwell in the house of the LORD forever."

SELAH—PAUSE AND REFLECT

On a scale of 1–10, with 1 being not very content at all and 10 being completely content, how would you rate your contentment at this point in time?

Consider the different aspects of your life: spiritual, relational (e.g., marriage, friendship, parenting, siblings, etc.), professional, emotional, and physical. In which aspect are you hoping to see God work in your heart in the area of contentment this week?

MEMORIZE: Psalm 23:1–2

LISTEN: "Shepherd" performed by Amanda Cook

POUR OUT YOUR HEART

Write a prayer to the Lord asking Him to shape you into a more contented person.

EVENING PRAISE

Lord Jesus, my Shepherd,

I praise You because in You I have all that I need.

I praise You that when I am discontent

You offer grace.

When I am fearful or sorrowful

You offer comfort.

When I am inadequate

You offer empowerment.

I praise You that You are faithful

and that You will perfect all that concerns me.

BASED ON PSALM 23:1, 4; 1 THESSALONIANS 5:24; PSALM 138:8

IT IS OFTEN A LONG HARD JOURNEY TO CONTENTMENT

MORNING PRAYER

Lord Jesus,

Your Word teaches me that godliness

with contentment is great gain.

Oh Lord, I realize I have so much farther to go

in this area of contentment.

Holy Spirit, please don't let up on me.

I pray that You would keep working on my attitude

and reshaping my will

until I am completely able to truly say,

It is well with my soul.

BASED ON 1 TIMOTHY 6:6

One of the most well-loved hymns of all times is "It Is Well with My Soul." The hymn was written by Horatio Spafford. He wrote the words after several traumatic events unfolded in his life. First, his four-year-old son died; then came the Chicago fire which brought financial ruin to Horatio. He and his family had planned a trip to Europe, but because of the circumstances and delays Horatio sent his family ahead on a ship. While crossing the ocean, the ship collided with another, and all four of Horatio's daughters died. Only his wife, Anna, survived. Honestly, I can't imagine so much grief. It was after Horatio received the news about his daughters that he penned the words to the majestic hymn.[5]

If there were ever words that described the true essence of contentment, it would be those words: "It is well with my soul." After losing everything, I dare say the little inconveniences of life didn't bother Horatio as much. He had found his comfort and peace in the presence of Christ.

Contentment doesn't mean we don't grieve. Grieving has an honored place in the believer's life. Jesus Himself grieved. It doesn't mean we fake being okay when we're not. It's doesn't mean we numb our pain to find peace in Netflix, chocolate cake, or alcohol. It means we are able to embrace sadness and sorrow, but we find calm in our understanding that God is good.

CONTENTMENT = CONFIDENT REST

It means we are satisfied with Jesus and rest in His love for us.

We experience peace in the truth that nothing and no one

compares to Him.

The path to contentment is outlined by David in Psalm 16. Let's take a look . . .

EXPLORE

READ PSALM 16

This is often called the Golden Psalm because it speaks prophetically of Jesus Christ. As we learn to focus on Jesus Christ, we discover that He alone is the source of our contentment.

What would you say is the overarching theme of this psalm?

READ PSALM 16:1

What is the desire David expressed in this first verse?

In verse 2, David uses two different Hebrew words for "Lord." The first is the Hebrew name for God, "Yahweh," which we talked about in week 1, day 5. Remember, this was the most proper name for God in the Hebrew language. The second word David uses for "Lord" is the Hebrew word *Adonai,* meaning "ruler."[6] In other words, David is saying, "Lord, You are the God of my forefathers and You are the Master of my life."

READ PSALM 16:2

David goes on to write, "Apart from you I have no good thing" (Ps. 16:2). How does the goodness of God compare to the goodness of other things?

How does David describe "holy people"?

David describes those who "run after other gods" (Ps. 16:4). What are some other gods that people run after in this present day and age?

READ PSALM 16:5

David writes that the Lord is his portion and his cup (Ps. 16:5). He uses references to food here. In other words, as John Piper writes, "If there are a hundred portions of food and drink spread out on the table, and one of them is the Lord himself—he is my choice. Nothing satisfies—nothing nourishes and sustains—the way he does."[7]

READ PSALM 16:6

Lots and lines are poetic descriptions of the land that was divided in ancient Israel. (Read Joshua 21:43–45.) When Joshua led the people of Israel into the promised land, the Lord divided the land between the tribes. When David writes in Psalm 16:6 that the lots and lines have fallen to him in pleasant places, he is referencing the divvying up of the land and the inheritance each tribe received. David is expressing gratitude that God Himself is his inheritance and that God always keeps His promises, as is evidenced in Joshua 21:43–45.

READ PSALM 16:9–11

What is the promise of living a contented life?

SELAH—PAUSE AND REFLECT

How would you define an idol?

What are some common idols that people worship today? List them below.

What would be some idols you might personally feel drawn to (e.g., money, beauty, security, etc.)?

How does comparing our life to the life of another encourage us to chase after idols?

How does comparing your life to the life of another create anxiety for you?

MEMORIZE: Psalm 23:1–2

LISTEN: **"Most Beautiful"** / "So in Love" (featuring Chandler Moore), Maverick City Music, Legendado

POUR OUT YOUR HEART

Write a prayer to the Lord pouring out your heart about a battle with comparing your circumstances to that of others.

EVENING PRAISE

Lord Jesus, I praise You that

because of Your love I can talk with You at any time.

I take refuge in You as I go to bed.

Spread Your protection over me as I sleep.

Let me fall asleep rejoicing in You.

BASED ON PSALM 5:7, 11

THE SOURCE OF SATISFACTION

MORNING PRAYER

Lord, my God,

I take refuge in You today.

Save me from my anxious thoughts.

Spring up in me a well of ever-flowing

satisfaction in You.

Teach me to focus on You

as my ultimate source of contentment.

BASED ON PSALM 7:1

As I write this, we are in the months of social distancing and quarantine. Thousands have died of the coronavirus. Many church services have moved online. Hundreds are grieving and thousands are scared. Protective masks and gloves have become our new normal. We are in the desert experience of a global pandemic. We will never forget this season of history, and it will forever change the way we live our lives. Desert experiences tend to do that.

In the desert, we dare to ask questions we might otherwise never ask. Questions like, "Where is God?" and "Why doesn't He step in and rescue us from our suffering?" "Is He really enough in this season?" Ah, seasons in the desert tempt us to either doubt God's goodness and provision, or they force us to cling more tightly to His faithfulness and love.

David was in the desert. Bible commentators are divided, but he was being chased and his life was threatened either by his own son, Absalom, or by King Saul. Nonetheless, whoever was threatening David, it forced him to hide in the wilderness. Exhausted and likely discouraged, David penned a song of worship. Turn in your Bible to Psalm 63. It is absolutely one of my favorites. It expresses David's deep longing for God, not just for protection but for God Himself.

EXPLORE

READ PSALM 63 OUT LOUD

David begins his worship song by using the name for God, *El*, which means "the strong One." What a great way to start your worship when you're feeling exhausted and weary. He then writes, "Earnestly I seek you; I thirst for you, my whole being longs for you, in a dry and parched land where there is no water." Here David uses a metaphor from his surroundings for how his soul feels.

READ PSALM 63:2

David reflects on a time when he had experienced the richness of God's presence. When we feel barren spiritually or emotionally, it is helpful to practice what I call the "worship of remembrance."

What does David remember in verse 2 that encourages his soul toward praise?

READ PSALM 63:3–4

How does David describe God's love in these verses?

His response is to "glorify" and praise God. The word that's used here for glorify is the Hebrew word *shabach*. It means "to commend, praise, or adore."[8] It seems to refer to speaking words of praise. He goes on to write, "In your name I will lift up my hands." When we lift our hands, it is an act of surrender. Not only do we praise God with our lips, but we also praise Him with our surrender. This is why people often raise their hands in church when worshiping.

READ PSALM 63:5

What do you think it means for the Lord to completely satisfy your soul?

How might deep satisfaction in the Lord heal the inner anxiety we often feel?

READ PSALM 63:6–11

As a result of his worship David makes several intentional choices. List David's choices below.

SELAH—PAUSE AND REFLECT

Often when we're exhausted, discouragement follows. In those moments, how might expressing praise and thanksgiving to God bring you to a more contented place?

In your life, when walking through seasons of loss or discouragement, when have you realized that Jesus is indeed enough? Reflect on that season and write your thoughts in the space below.

MEMORIZE: Write out Psalm 23:1–2 from memory.

LISTEN: "First Love" sung by Kari Jobe

POUR OUT YOUR HEART

Write a prayer to the Lord describing what it has felt like for you to be in a desert. Express your longing for Him.

EVENING PRAISE

I will give thanks to You, Lord.

Thank You for the blessings that I experienced today

because of Your righteousness.

As I wind down this evening,

I will sing the praises of the name

of the Lord Most High.

I praise You for Your love and faithfulness.

BASED ON PSALMS 7:17; 115:1

WHERE'S YOUR FOCUS?

MORNING PRAYER

Lord Jesus,

I lift my eyes to You this morning;

You are the one who sits enthroned in the heavens.

Help me to keep my eyes focused on You today.

BASED ON PSALM 123:1

My daughter Stefanie had had a rough day, emotionally. As she headed to bed that night, she discovered a note from her eight-year-old daughter, Selah. The note said, "Um, Mom, will you memorize Hebrews 12:2 with me?" Selah's note was profound and brought comfort and a smile to Stef's heart. Basically, sweet Selah was saying, "Mom, let's shift our focus." Wow! The wisdom of a child. Right?! When life is difficult and demanding, we need to refocus our attention on the Lord.

Today I want us to revisit Psalm 16 and Psalm 63 with the emphasis on *where* we focus.

EXPLORE

What do these psalms have in common as far as David's focus?

Circle the words, "I keep my eyes always on the LORD." How does keeping his eyes on the Lord impact David's emotions?

David references his mind and his body in both psalms. What impact does keeping his focus on the Lord have on David's body? On his mind? On his heart?

In Acts 2:25–28, the apostle Peter quotes David from Psalm 16. This points to the prophetic element of what David was writing. Who was David prophesying about?

READ ACTS 2:28

What does this say about Jesus Christ and our ability to experience His presence? How does the presence of Christ calm our souls and bring contentment?

SELAH—PAUSE AND REFLECT

READ HEBREWS 12:1–2

These verses teach that we are to have a fixed focus. In other words, an undistracted focus. How might fixing your eyes on Jesus help quiet anxiety in your day-to-day life? How might it fill you with deeper contentment?

How does comparing yourself to others create anxiety for you and distract you from Jesus?

MEMORIZE: Review Psalm 23:1–2

LISTEN: "No Other Love" as performed by Jake Espy, Red Rocks Worship Acoustic

POUR OUT YOUR HEART

Write out a prayer to the Lord about the difficulties and demands you are facing at this time.

EVENING PRAISE

Lord Jesus,
I center my focus on You as I end my day.
I praise You that You are enthroned in heaven.
As I sleep, Your loving hand protects and preserves me.
Thank You that I can sleep in peace, knowing
You have all the concerns and circumstances of my life
under control.

BASED ON PSALM 123:1; 4:8

THE CALMING REST OF HIS PRESENCE

MORNING PRAYER

Lord God, You are my God,
I'm thirsty for more of You today.
As I come before You at the beginning of this new morning,
help me to focus on You as the source of my satisfaction.
You are the one who said that those who set their hope on You
will lack nothing.
Fill me with Your Holy Spirit today.

BASED ON PSALMS 63:1; 84:11

Over the past 15–20 years, I have put effort into scheduling at least one day a month as a day of prayer and personal reflection. My goal? To simply enjoy God's presence. Those days have become a treasure on my calendar. There in His presence I am able to let go of tension and stress and just simply rest in God's deep abiding love for me. As I contentedly linger in God's presence, He revives, restores, and renews my soul.

Psalm 84 is a song of praise for God's presence. The theme is the joy and contentment that is found in the presence of God. In Israel, pilgrims often journeyed to the temple to celebrate and worship God. As they made their way into the synagogue, they often sang the words of Psalm 84. If you're going to live a life of contentment, you need to learn to enjoy God's presence because it is in His presence that the greatest satisfaction comes. Open your Bible to Psalm 84.

EXPLORE

READ PSALM 84 OUT LOUD

READ PSALM 84:1–2

How are these verses similar to Psalm 63:1–2?

READ PSALM 84:3

What pictures of contentment does the psalmist paint here?

Often through the Scriptures the word "blessed" means happy or contented. The psalmist writes, "Blessed are those who dwell in your house." That word "dwell" makes me think of nestling down and being at home in the presence of God. It's the sense that He is with me 24/7.

Brother Lawrence was a sixteenth-century monk who lived in France. "He resolved to live in continual awareness of God's presence, to never forget him from one moment to the next."[9] As a result of cultivating mindfulness of God in every moment of life, Brother Lawrence enjoyed great contentment. When we learn to delight in God's abiding presence, He satisfies our souls.

READ PSALM 84:5-7

The person who sets their heart on knowing God's presence more intimately finds immeasurable strength. As we luxuriate in God's presence, the Holy Spirit strengthens our souls. As a result, even the valley of *Baka*, which commentators have called "the valley of tears,"[10] can become a place of blessing. It's not that we enjoy walking through the valley of tears; it's that as we walk in deep intimacy with God through that valley, He pours immeasurable strength into our souls.

How might suffering serve the greater purpose of strengthening us when we determine to make God's presence our home?

David prays for favor from the Lord. Do you think praying for favor is compatible with contentment?

What is the promise given in Psalm 84:11 to those who delight in enjoying God's presence?

In week 2, we read about the time David wanted to build the temple but God said no. How does this passage reflect a heart of contentment even when God withheld something David thought was good?

At the time when this story took place, David was an old man. But he had spent countless hours praising and worshiping God. His response to God's no demonstrates, more than any other action of his, the extraordinary power of praise to bring contentment to our lives.

SELAH—PAUSE AND REFLECT

What practices do you put in place to enjoy God's presence?

In what areas of life have you experienced the valley of tears? How might those times have become a place of blessing in your life?

In what areas of life are you praying for favor from the Lord? How can you cultivate contentment as you wait for His answer?

MEMORIZE: Review Psalm 23:1–2

LISTEN: "On Earth as It Is in Heaven" performed by Red Rocks Worship

POUR OUT YOUR HEART

Write a prayer to the Lord expressing your desire to experience more of His presence and power in your life.

EVENING PRAISE

I praise You this evening, Lord.
I glorify You for who You are.
I praise You that Your presence is with me at every moment.
Thank You that Your desire is for my presence as well.
Your love is better than life to me.

BASED ON PSALM 63:4–5

REKINDLING EXUBERANT JOY

RETURNING AND RESTORATION

MORNING PRAYER

Father God, I praise You that my help today

is in the name of the Lord.

I lay down at Your feet

every worry, anxiety, concern, and care.

I ask that Your peace would rule in my heart and mind today.

I pray peace over my household and family.

I pray peace over my mind and thinking.

I pray peace over all who I will encounter today.

May You be lifted high in my life.

BASED ON PSALM 124:8; 122:7–8

As I write this, the coronavirus pandemic continues. Social distancing and mask wearing are our new normal. Apparently, according to last night's news, there's no end in sight. With the pandemic and isolation, anxiety and depression are on the rise. Our nation and other nations around the world are tired. People are worried about their loved ones, and some are dying without family members close by due to hospital restrictions. On top of all that, there is political polarization, wonky weather patterns, fire ravishing many places, and an economy teetering on the brink of collapse. Basically, our lives have been turned upside-down! For those in our generation, we've never seen a global crisis of this magnitude.

How do we as followers of Jesus stay joyful in such chaotic times? I believe praise is key! This week we're going to look at the extraordinary power of praise to release joy in our lives, even when life is difficult.

EXPLORE

READ PSALM 126 OUT LOUD

This psalm is one of the Psalms of Ascent (Psalm 120 through 134). When Steve and I were visiting Israel, our guide told us that the Psalms of Ascent were sung by the Levite priests as they processed up the fifteen steps to the temple. Imagine the chorus of praise as the priests called others to worship as they marched up the steps. Wow! What a way to start your worship service, right?!

Other Bible commentators say that the Psalms of Ascent were sung by pilgrims coming to Jerusalem for worship. Perhaps both are true—joyful singing from those entering the city for worship and joy-filled singing of the priests ascending the steps to the temple.

In this particular psalm, the words reflect a joy-filled return after years of exile in Babylon. The song helps the children of Israel remember the great joy of returning and the joy of restoration. Restoration of broken dreams, restoration of financial loss, restoration of hearts coming back home to the Lord.

The psalmist teaches us three principles of joy: **God has rescued us from captivity, God has restored what's been lost, God will renew our strength for the future.** As you read, look for these three principles. The Word of God is eternal, so though this is a psalm that was sung joyfully by worshipers entering the temple, the principles apply to you today!

READ PSALM 126

What did God restore for the people of Israel according to this psalm?

READ PSALM 126:2-3

Write down the three distinct ways the people expressed themselves in their celebration:

1.

2.

3.

READ PSALM 126:5–6

What is the promise about sowing and reaping a harvest that is found in these verses?

READ PSALM 126

List all the expressions of joy.

SELAH—PAUSE AND REFLECT

In what areas of life has God rescued you from captivity, restored what's been lost, and renewed your strength? How have you praised God in that process? Write your thoughts in the space below.

Do you think laughter should be a part of our worship and praise? Why or why not?

The word "restoration" implies the action of restoring something to its original beauty or returning something to its rightful owner. In what areas of your life do you need restoration? What action steps do you need to take to move forward toward restoration?

READ PSALM 126:5–6

Consider your own life. In what areas of your life do you need to sow more seed in order to achieve more joy and soul satisfaction?

What does this psalm speak to you personally about joy?

MEMORIZE: Write out Psalm 96:1–3 and begin to commit it to memory.

LISTEN: "Joy of the Lord" performed by Rend Collective

POUR OUT YOUR HEART

Write out a prayer to the Lord asking Him to increase your joy.

EVENING PRAISE

Lord Jesus, I praise You that Your desire

for me is to have Your joy.

Not just a little bit of joy, but fullness of joy!

Thank You that You are the source of all joy,

and that as I nurture my relationship with You

my gladness grows.

I praise You for the moments of laughter I've had today

as well as the moments when I've been challenged.

I praise You that Your

joy has been my strength through this past day.

I exalt You, Lord Jesus!

I praise You that as I rest,

You will fill my heart with joy!

BASED ON JOHN 15:11; NEHEMIAH 8:10

GRATITUDE UNLEASHES A TSUNAMI OF JOY

MORNING PRAYER

Good morning, Lord!
As my heart, soul, and body wake up,
fill me with a heart of gratitude.
Lord, Your word says, "Give thanks to the Lord,
for He is good."
Help me as I move through my day
to stop often and give You thanks.
Press down into my heart Your goodness
when doubt comes my way;
Help me to silence the voice of the enemy
by singing about Your goodness.
My heart is grateful that You will be with me
every moment of this new day.

BASED ON PSALM 107:1, 8; 143:12

Steve and I started a new practice a couple of years ago during an intense season of ministry. The challenges of ministry were great and we found ourselves battling discouragement. We bought a journal and put it in the napkin holder on our table. Every night at dinner, when we're home, we write down the top three blessings of our days. It's been remarkable to think back over each day—with all the challenges—and list three blessings for each of us. Sometimes our blessings are not huge. We might list a wonderful conversation with one of our kids or a snuggle from a grandchild. We might list a rejuvenating hike or the beauty of the mountains. We might list an encouraging email or a life-giving phone call. Whatever the blessing, when we focus and give thanks, our hearts are lifted and we feel filled with joy. Gratitude unleashes a tsunami of joy in our souls and this is part of why it is such an important element of worship.

EXPLORE

READ PSALM 95 OUT LOUD

Then read the psalm again slowly. What expressions or postures of praise do you see in this psalm? List them:

The word for "thanksgiving" that's used here is from the Hebrew word *todah*, which means "thanks, thanksgiving, adoration, praise." The word is derived from the verb *yadah*, "to give thanks, to praise." The root of *yadah* is *yad,* "hand."[1] To thank or praise God is to lift our hands in thanks to Him. Now you might feel embarrassed to lift your hands in worship. Perhaps you could lift your hands in worship when you are home, in your private worship setting. The lifting of our hands is not only a powerful symbol of gratitude but also the universal sign of surrender. In our worship, we bring our gratitude and surrender our expectations. Ah, sit with that thought for just a moment and ponder how profound that is!

My goal is to broaden your knowledge of how Scripture describes worship. In 2 Samuel 6:14, David does more than raise his hands. Wearing only a linen ephod, he danced before the Lord "with all his might." His wife Michal mocked him for his outburst. But David assured her . . . he could become even more undignified (vv. 21–22)! Let me pause for just a moment and ask you, when was the last time you danced for joy before the Lord? God is delighted with our uninhibited and undignified worship!

How might trying some new expressions and postures of praise renew your joy?

How does thanksgiving and gratitude in general affect the human mind?

How does music help us extol the Lord?

READ PSALM 95:3-5

How does the psalmist describe the Lord in these verses? How is describing the Lord's characteristics an act of worship?

READ PSALM 95:6-7

Why is kneeling before the Lord an important posture of worship? What does this signify?

The psalmist makes reference to the Lord being our shepherd and writes, "We are the people of his pasture, the flock under his care" (Ps. 95:7). This is a similar picture to the one David paints in Psalm 23:1–2. A shepherd never led his sheep to a bad pasture; doing so would mean the sheep would die. This is a reference to the shepherd's loving provision.

In the New Testament, Jesus said He was the "good Shepherd" (John 10:11). What does this speak about the character of God? How does knowing that the Lord is your Good Shepherd help to quiet anxiety?

READ PSALM 95:8–11

At first, this seems like a very awkward ending to a psalm of praise. But as you explore the reference to the waters of Meribah found in Exodus 17, you realize that it is a reference to the children of Israel not trusting in God's provision in the wilderness. They complained, doubted God's goodness, and basically dreamed of going back to Egypt, where they had been in captivity. The lesson for us as the people of God is pretty clear. When life gets tough, it can become tempting to doubt the Lord's goodness and presence. However, if instead we choose to praise God and trust Him by faith, the rewards are huge. We find joy and peace, and we experience His presence in deeper ways.

The question is how? How do we authentically praise and trust God, while still struggling with the fear that God has forgotten us? **The key is in praising Him by faith! As you do, the Holy Spirit awakens deeper trust in your heart**.

Friend, I can't tell you how many early mornings I have gotten on my knees with a heart full of anxiety, fear, or sadness as I've begun my worship time. As I have praised God by faith, no matter my circumstances, He has met me. Whether sweltering in Africa, kneeling on a cement floor, or freezing in Central Asia, whether surrounded by danger or peacefully at home, God has transformed my anxiety into joy. That is the extraordinary power of praise! The truth is you cannot praise God authentically and not be changed!

The next time you feel doubt moving in on you, get down on your knees. Yes, bow and begin to praise God for every character trait you can think of. Turn on some worship music and allow the music to focus your heart on Almighty God. Watch and see how your attitude changes. I believe you will experience joy that you never thought was possible!

SELAH—PAUSE AND REFLECT

Do you feel comfortable in worship services where people raise their hands or shout in praise? Why or why not?

How have thanksgiving and cultivating a heart of gratitude been helpful to you in your worship journey? How have they been helpful in cultivating a heart of joy?

Has there ever been a time when you have been going through what felt like a wilderness experience, where you have been tempted to doubt God's goodness? Write about that experience below.

Start keeping a gratitude journal and every night, either after dinner or before bed, write down your top three blessings of the day.

MEMORIZE: Review Psalm 96:1–3

LISTEN: "Grateful" performed by Elevation Worship

POUR OUT YOUR HEART

Write a prayer to the Lord in the space below, asking Him to increase your gratefulness.

EVENING PRAISE

I exalt You, Lord Jesus!

You are a good and faithful God.

Thank You for the blessings of this day_____

[List three blessings].

I praise You for moments of unexpected joy.

You are a good God whose faithfulness can't be measured.

Thank You for Your faithfulness over my life.

I praise You that even in times when life has felt difficult,

Your presence has never left me.

Thank You that You are the One who fills my heart with joy.

BASED ON PSALM 33:4; 95:2; 139:7

PRAISING GOD WITH MUSIC

MORNING PRAYER

Lord Jesus, good morning!

The whole earth is filled with Your glory this morning.

I praise You that whenever morning dawns

and evening fades,

You call me to sing songs of praise.

You answer me when I call;

You are the hope of all the earth.

Thank You that I don't have to move through my day isolated.

Your presence goes with me,

in front of me, and behind me,

above me and beneath me.

Help me today to continually come into Your presence

with songs of joy and hope.

BASED ON PSALM 65:8, 5; 139:5; 100:1-2

Praising God can take a lot of different forms. Certainly there's a place for creating a thankful list when life is falling apart or for declaring God's amazing attributes. But there's also an honored place for worship music.

Music brings celebrations to life. In case you're wondering, in heaven there will be music (Rev. 5:8–9; 14:3–4). You might not be able to sing on key, but the great thing about God is that He hears in perfect pitch.

The bottom line is that music was designed by God to be a part of our worship experience with Him. At times the music is quiet and reflective, drawing us into quiet worship, and at other times it's loud and celebrative. Sometimes, we worship to old ancient hymns and sometimes to worship songs newly released. Both traditional and contemporary music have a place in our worship. Here's truth, my friend—neither is more "spiritual" than the other. One might lead *you* deeper into worship than the other, but for someone else it could be the opposite. In our worship we must guard against judging the style preference of others. No matter what style of music you prefer, allow the music to prompt you to deeper worship.

Today we're going to look at how music can enhance your worship. I'm going to have you flip through and look up several verses in the Psalms and a few in the New Testament to show you God's heart for music. Hey, grab your Bible, and let's get started.

EXPLORE

Look up the following passages. Next to each, write what you feel the verses are teaching and what each speaks to you personally:

Psalm 96:1–2

Psalm 71:23

Psalm 98:1–2

Psalm 101:1

Psalm 135:3

Ephesians 5:19

What part does worship music play in rekindling our joy?

SELAH—PAUSE AND REFLECT

Do you use worship music in the time you spend with Jesus? Why or why not?

In what ways might worship music be a useful tool to help prompt your praise? Have you ever listened to worship music when you have felt sad? How has the music impacted you emotionally?

When you are at church, do you find yourself engaged in the worship music or distracted by the music? What is God speaking to you through this?

MEMORIZE: Write out Psalm 96:1–3.

LISTEN: List three of your favorite songs of worship in the space below. Then get on your knees and listen to each song either on your phone or computer. Allow the music to prompt your praise. When you're finished, write in the space below your reflections on what you experienced as far as God's presence.

Here's one of my favorite worship songs: "O Praise the Name (Anastasis)" by Hillsong Worship

POUR OUT YOUR HEART

Write your thoughts in the form of a prayer about music and your feelings about worship music.

EVENING PRAISE

Lord, as I close out this day,

let me go to bed with a song of praise on my heart.

I praise You and thank You for the gift of music.

As I rest in You and sing in the shadow of Your wings,

fill my heart and soul with songs of hope and deliverance.

May I face tomorrow morning with a new song on my lips.

I praise You that You delight in me

and that Your presence watches over me as I sleep.

BASED ON PSALM 63:7; 32:7; 147:11

EXUBERANT PRAISE = EXUBERANT JOY

MORNING PRAYER

Good morning, Lord!

I lift my eyes up to You.

You are enthroned above the heavens and the earth.

I bow low before You

and wait for You to speak to me.

Holy Spirit, move in my heart

so that I delight to not only be in Your presence,

but I delight in doing Your will.

May my joy be abundantly full

as I keep my eyes focused on You today.

BASED ON PSALM 123:1–2; 40:8 (NLT)

God has wired you for worship and praising Him. Why? Is He some egotistical God who constantly needs His ego propped up with an attaboy? No. He designed you for worship because as you worship Him, you are changed! The more you worship and praise God, the more you become like Him and the more you are filled with joy.

Dr. Carolyn Leaf, a cognitive neuroscientist specializing in cognitive and metacognitive neuropsychology, teaches that "when we thank, praise, and worship God, we prime our circuits for high intellectual function and every cell in our body is positively affected."[2] As a result, joy and gladness increase, and anxiety and depression decrease. How does this happen? I could try to explain it scientifically, but honestly, I'm not going to try. Science is merely just backing up what God has said all along, and that's that you were designed to worship Him! It therefore makes total sense that if you're doing what you're designed to do, joy and gladness will rise up in you.

I believe as you rise above your circumstances with exuberant praise, exuberant joy will also rise.

EXPLORE

READ PSALM 100 OUT LOUD

Write out Psalm 100:1–2 in the space below. Circle the words "joy" and "gladness."

How would you define joy?

How would you define gladness?

The word for worship that's used in Psalm 100:2 is the Hebrew word *abad*, and it means "to work for, serve, do labor for someone; to be a servant; to worship."[3] The verbal root of this word is *ebed*, "servant." A servant is a person who does the bidding of His master. The greatest example we have of this is Jesus, who is called a servant of the Lord by the prophet Isaiah (Isa. 53:11). Jesus did the absolute will of the Father by going to the cross.

In what ways is our worship and exuberant praise an act of service to the Lord?

READ PSALM 100:3

Sheep belong to their shepherd. They know the shepherd and follow him. In what ways do we as sheep follow and obey our Shepherd as an act of worship?

Circle the word "praise."

The word for praise that's used here is the Hebrew word *tehillah*. It means "a celebration, a lauding of someone praiseworthy; the praise or exaltation of God; praise songs of admiration."[4] The Hebrew word for the book of Psalms is actually *Tehillim*, meaning book of praises!

An exuberant celebration is implied with this word. This implies a party hearty, throw-your-hands-in-the-air, shout and stomp your feet kind of praise. It's almost like being at the Super Bowl when your team wins. Do you stand there calmly and clap? Nope. You jump in the air; you scream and shout and cheer your heart out. That's the kind of praise this is talking about! Try being a little exuberant in your praise! You'll be shocked at how joy rises!

READ AND WRITE OUT PSALM 100:5

Wow! Did you catch that? The Lord is *good*! His love endures *forever*! His faithfulness continues through *all generations*! Sit with those words for a minute or two. Hey, the God you serve is good; I mean really good! He will never stop loving you. He will continue to be faithful to your children and grandchildren and your great-grandchildren. Celebrate!

SELAH—PAUSE AND REFLECT

What has this psalm taught you about how we enter into God's presence?

Would you describe your natural bent as more of a pessimist or an enthusiast? How does your natural personality affect your worship and praise?

Do you gravitate more toward quiet reflective worship or loud exuberant praise? Both are wonderful in God's eyes.

What gives you the most joy in your worship of the Lord?

MEMORIZE: Psalm 96:1–3

LISTEN: "You and You Alone" sung by Rheva Henry, Bethel Worship

POUR OUT YOUR HEART

Write a prayer to the Lord describing to Him when you feel His presence most closely.

EVENING PRAISE

Oh Lord, I praise You because You are

good, holy, faithful, loving, and kind.

You are worthy of all my praise and thanksgiving.

As I end this day,

I bring You a heart of gratitude.

I leave every care in Your hands.

I praise You in advance for the rest You will give.

Thank You for your abiding presence.

May Your blessing be on my family,

even my children's children.

BASED ON PSALM 100:5; 95:2; 103:17

JOYFUL CELEBRATION

MORNING PRAYER

Lord Jesus, I praise You for a new morning!
I praise You for the strength You will give me today.
Thank You that each new day brings a new opportunity to
celebrate Your goodness.
Thank You that You have invited me to find joy in You.
You are the source and the supplier of all joy.
It is Your very nature to be joy, and
as I praise You and become a partaker of Your nature
I am filled with joy as well.

BASED ON PSALM 59:16; 145:7

When my kids were little, birthdays and holidays in our home were a big deal. Balloons, party napkins, cupcakes, and candy were all included. I loved celebrations and hosting parties for my kids. Now that I have grandkids, I often will have a birthday sleepover for that particular grandchild.

Recently, my grandson, Ty, turned ten. I invited two of his cousins and treated them to go-cart racing. Then we had pizza for dinner, and the boys had what they called an "epic sleepover." That evening there was lots of laughter and fun as the boys settled in for the night. Ty later wrote about that sleepover in a paragraph he had to write for school on when he experienced joy.

The Hebrew word for "celebrate" comes from a root word meaning "to laugh."[5] We often think of God as being all serious and somber. But if you read about Jesus in the gospels, you'll discover that Jesus loved a good party. He used humor in His stories and enjoyed a good laugh.

David calls us to celebrative worship in Psalm 149. It's not that He's saying you have to laugh while you worship—although God enjoys the sound of your laughter—it's that He's calling for exuberant celebration!

EXPLORE

READ PSALM 149 OUT LOUD

READ PSALM 149 SILENTLY

Circle any word that speaks of joy in worship.

READ PSALM 149:1

Why do you think the psalmist instructs us to sing a "new song" as a part of our praise?

READ PSALM 149:2

In your Bible, circle the words, "Rejoice in their Maker." We've studied joy all week. How would you say worshiping and praising God releases joy in our lives?

READ PSALM 149:3

The phrase "make music" here is the Hebrew word *zamar*, which means "to make music, singing praises, to sing songs accompanied by musical instruments."[6] It paints the picture for us of a grand musical celebration.

In your opinion, how do musical instruments assist in our celebration?

READ PSALM 149:4

God delights in our exuberant worship. It's crazy, right? What is the promise contained in this verse for those who humble themselves to worship the Lord exuberantly?

How is worship a humbling experience?

READ PSALM 149:5

The psalmist instructs us to sing for joy on our beds. How might worship music help you sleep better at night?

READ PSALM 149:6–9

I often pray for my grandkids, "May the praise of God be in their mouths and a double-edged sword in their hands." How might using the weapons of praising God and declaring Scripture help defeat the enemy of depression or anxiety in your life?

SELAH—PAUSE AND REFLECT

Think back on the studies we've done this past week. Praising God is key to experiencing true joy. Spend a few moments reflecting on what God has spoken to your heart this past week.

How might you incorporate worship music into time with Jesus every day?

On a daily basis, how do you keep joy at the forefront of your thinking? How important to you is it that your home is filled with joy? What most often detracts from joy in your home?

What steps do you need to take moving forward to become a more joy-filled person?

MEMORIZE: Write Psalm 96:1–3 from memory in the space below.

LISTEN: "Come Alive (Live)" by Red Rocks Worship

POUR OUT YOUR HEART

Write out a prayer in the space below asking the Lord to fill your heart and your home with joy. If there's any specific thing that comes to mind that is blocking your joy, ask the Lord for wisdom for how to move past that.

EVENING PRAISE

Lord, I praise You that You are the joy-giver

and You call me to rejoice.

As I think back on my day,

I praise You for the moments _____

[fill in with specifics]

when I felt Your presence so close.

I praise You for the times_____ [fill in specifics]

when I needed wisdom and You gave it.

I praise You that as I rest this evening

my heart can be filled with joy,

because You are good and everything You do is good.

I praise You that as I sleep

You will sing over me with songs of joy.

BASED ON PHILIPPIANS 4:4; PSALM 145:9; ZEPHANIAH 3:17

LIVING IN VICTORY

THE PROCESSION OF VICTORY

MORNING PRAYER

Lord Jesus, You are my victor.
As I move through this day,
tune my ear to Your words of victory.
Help me to remember that nothing can
stand in the way of Your awesome power.
Chase away all my fears.
Empower me to rise up with courage today.
May Your favor rest upon me today.
Let my mouth overflow with highest praise.
Fill me with joy in Your presence
as I stand in victory today.

BASED ON PSALM 90:17

My sweet granddaughter, Selah, loves the Fourth of July. Every year we go to the parade that's hosted in our community. Honestly, it's an epic parade, especially for small-town America. In addition to bands playing patriotic themes, the parade includes elephants, ponies with horns on their heads to look like unicorns, pirates, and all manner of floats.

Candy is thrown from the parade, and booths and concession stands line the side streets in the center of town. We do all the things. Selah gets her face painted—red, white, and blue, of course. She gets her hair braided and decorated with glitter. She collects all manner of free items being given away: red, white, and blue sunglasses, bracelets, stickers, and a host of other goodies. The local church hosts a pancake breakfast, and Selah usually ends up being interviewed by our local news, probably because she's so cute! It's such a fun morning for our sweet grandkids.

Psalm 68 describes a triumphant parade led by none other than our victorious Jesus! Written by David, it is a song of celebration and victory.

EXPLORE

READ PSALM 68:1-3

The psalm begins echoing the cry of Moses evoking the blessing of God over the Israelites as they fled from Egypt: "Rise up, Lord! May your enemies be scattered; may your foes flee before you" (Num. 10:35). You remember the story. The cloud of the Lord was over the Israelites by day, shielding them from the heat of the day, and the pillar of fire by night as they journeyed through the wilderness. God's presence led them every step of the way in their journey through the barren desert. Every morning as the ark would go in front leading the people, Moses would cry, "Rise up, Lord!" The shekinah glory of God led His people out of captivity. David wrote a song that remembered and celebrated that victorious march.

Circle in your Bible the words "happy and joyful." How might singing the praises of the Lord who gives victory bring you happiness personally? How might the practice of singing and worship defeat the enemy and help bring victory in your life?

READ PSALM 68:5-6

David lists several specific reasons to praise and extol the Lord in these two verses. List some of the specific reasons in the space below:

READ PSALM 68:7-10 AND NUMBERS 11:1-20

David recounts the victorious march from Mount Sinai and how God provided for His people. In what ways did God provide not only for the people but also specifically for Moses as he led the people?

In these verses, David celebrates the victory won by the Lord. This may also be a prophetic reference to the cross of Christ where our victory was won over sin. We who are in Christ are now made whiter than the snow that has fallen on Mount Zalmon.

From your perspective, why is it important for you as a believer to celebrate that Christ has won victory over sin for you?

READ PSALM 68:19–23

In what way did Jesus Christ crush Satan under His feet? How does He deliver us from death? The following verses may help you answer these two questions. Write your thoughts next to each one.

Romans 16:20

John 5:24

SELAH—PAUSE AND REFLECT

READ PSALM 68:24-25

The apostle Paul writes similarly in 2 Corinthians 2:14 that Jesus leads us as captives in triumphant procession. In both ancient Israel and in Ancient Rome, when battles were won the winning general would lead a parade through the streets, parading the captives from the battle. In our lives it is Jesus Christ, the Righteous One, who leads us as His captives, who have been freed from sin and shame.

In what areas of your life has Jesus led you triumphantly out of captivity? Write your thoughts in the space below. Be specific. Then spend time praising God for each and every victory He has won in your life.

MEMORIZE: Psalm 68:26

LISTEN: "Underneath My Feet (Live)" by Red Rocks Worship

POUR OUT YOUR HEART

Write a prayer in the space below about a place in your life where you need to experience victory.

EVENING PRAISE

Lord, I praise You that Your glorious presence
has led me victoriously through this day.
I praise You that even during the rougher moments of my day
You were there to lead and guide me.
Your presence never left me.
I praise You that You daily carry my burdens.
Thank You that I can trust You to be with me tomorrow.
Lord, I praise You in Your awesome sanctuary.

BASED ON PSALM 68:24; 139:7; 68:19, 3

PRAISING GOD UNLEASHES VICTORY IN YOUR LIFE

MORNING PRAYER

My Sovereign Lord, I bow before You today.

I long to abide in Your presence as I move through my day.

I thank You that Your Holy Spirit never leaves me.

He is my 24/7 journey mate,

to equip and empower me to walk in victory.

Help me to tune my ear to You, listening today for Your voice.

Bring my heart and will into perfect alignment with Yours.

May I proclaim with my mouth Your wonders

and may my life declare Your power this day.

BASED ON PSALM 68:20, 34; JOHN 14:15

The other day, I was chatting with several friends throughout my day. Every friend has either had a lot of health issues and challenges, or they've had a family member experience those challenges. I noticed a common theme in my conversations. Each one of my friends was walking through dark and discouraging circumstances.

However, although they were authentic about their battle with discouragement, each one talked about how time spent worshiping God and remembering His goodness lifted their spirits and gave them victory over discouragement. That is the extraordinary power of praise!

EXPLORE

READ PSALM 68:26

Why is it important to praise God with others rather than just individually?

READ PSALM 68:27

You might be wondering, "What is David writing about?" Here's a little background: Benjamin, Judah, and Naphtali were all tribes of Israel. At different times in Israel's history the tribes did not get along with each other. However, when the people of God come together to praise Him, it brings about a supernatural unity within the body of Christ. When we are focused on praising God, we are not looking at each other critically. Rather, like Paul wrote in Romans 15:5–6, our mindset is changed:

> *May the God who gives endurance and encouragement*
> *give you the same attitude of mind toward each other*
> *that Christ Jesus had, so that with one mind and one voice*
> *you may glorify the God and Father of our Lord Jesus Christ.*

Unity in the body of Christ is a big deal to God. When we come together and we celebrate and praise God for the victories He has won for each of us, the blessing of unity pours out. David alludes to the unity between the tribes as they praise and worship God together.

Why is unity important in the church today?

READ PSALM 68:28

Here David cries out to God to display His might and power once again. It is a prayer that is in keeping with the heart of God. As David has worshiped and praised God, the Holy Spirit prompts his heart to pray for what's on the heart of God. The extraordinary power of praise is that as we praise and worship God, He in turn brings our hearts into alignment with His and we begin to cry out for the things that God wants us to ask for.

PSALM 68:29-31

One of the prayers of worship that God loves to answer is for Him to crush the enemy under our feet. We are given all authority in Jesus' name, and just as Jesus crushed Satan through His death and resurrection, we have died to our sin and are resurrected to new life in Christ. We are assured victory and so a part of our praise and worship is agreeing with God that He crushed the enemy who is trying to destroy the church.

READ PSALM 68:32-35

David instructs not only Israel but also the body of Christ to sing praises to the Lord. We were designed to worship and praise Him. We are to proclaim His glorious power to the world. What are some practical ways that worship helps us proclaim to the world God's goodness?

SELAH—PAUSE AND REFLECT

David ends his song of praise by reminding us that God is a God of power who gives strength to His people. In what areas of your life do you need strength at this present moment?

How might praising God renew your strength and hope in the victory that is yours?

MEMORIZE: Psalm 68:26

LISTEN: "There Is a Power" performed by Rita Springer / Dante Bowe

POUR OUT YOUR HEART

Write a prayer to the Lord expressing your need for His power in your life today.

EVENING PRAISE

Lord Jesus, I praise you that I have all authority in Your name.

Thank You that You have promised me victory

over the enemy as I trust You by faith.

In all things, I can be more than a conqueror.

I praise You that through Your name

I can trample on my enemies.

Tonight, I praise You

that I can lay down and sleep in peace,

knowing that You fight for me even

as I remain still.

BASED ON 1 JOHN 5:4; ROMANS 8:37; PSALM 44:5; 4:8; EXODUS 14:14

ANOTHER TRIUMPHANT MARCH

MORNING PRAYER

Lord Jesus, I praise You because You are victory!

I thank You because You promise me victory as I trust in You.

Today when I feel surrounded,

overwhelmed, or fearful,

remind me to praise and thank You for who You are,

above my circumstances.

Show me when I don't know what to do

to turn my eyes toward You.

Help me to remember today

that Your love endures forever.

BASED ON 1 CORINTHIANS 15:57; 2 CHRONICLES 20:12; PSALM 136:1

Have you ever felt surrounded on every side? Yup. I'm guessing you have. At different points in your life it feels as though you are being hit on every side with problems and difficulties.

I remember a time where it felt like I was surrounded on every side, and I felt pretty sure I was going to sink. Family problems, financial problems, and health problems all surrounded me. I felt paralyzed by difficulties and I remember crying out to the Lord, "Oh Lord, I don't know what to do, but my eyes are on You. Show me what to do next."

King Jehoshaphat felt similarly. Let's take a look at the story. Open your Bible to 2 Chronicles 20.

READ 2 CHRONICLES 20:1-30

After King Solomon's death (around 930 BC) the nation of Israel split in two. The northern part of the kingdom kept the name "Israel" while the southern part took the name Judah. Interestingly enough, the name Judah means "praised."[1] This story found in 2 Chronicles 20 is of the Southern part of the Kingdom, Judah.

Write a synopsis of this story in your own words in the space below, including the points that seem most essential to the story.

Then read the story again. **As you read, circle the following phrases in your Bible:**

- Alarmed, Jehoshaphat resolved to inquire of the LORD (v. 3).

- Power and might are in your hand (v. 6).

- We do not know what to do, but our eyes are on you (v. 12).

- Do not be afraid or discouraged (v. 15).

- The battle is not yours, but God's (v. 15).

- Take up your positions; stand firm (v. 17).

- Have faith (v. 20).

- As they began to sing and praise, the LORD set ambushes (v. 22).

After you circle those phrases, **write a few sentences reflecting on what God taught you through this story.**

Is this story applicable for believers today? Why or why not?

READ PSALM 136:1

Write out the verse here.

We don't know who wrote this psalm. It may have been David or someone else, but the people of Judah knew the song and had obviously committed it to memory. As the people of God marched out to fight the surrounding enemies they sang, "Give thanks to the LORD, for He is good. His love endures forever."

This is such a profound response to troubles, trials, and threats. In our culture there is such a high priority on being authentic, and rightly so. In your opinion, do you think it is authentic to praise God when you are completely overwhelmed with problems? Why or why not?

As the people of God praised God, what happened to their fear? What evidence do you find for your answer?

SELAH—PAUSE AND REFLECT

When you are alarmed or feel afraid, how can you transition to praise in your thinking?

How does praising God and giving thanks bring victory into your life? Why do you think we so often forget this principle?

What action steps do you need to take as a result of today's lesson?

MEMORIZE: Psalm 68:26

LISTEN: "Reign Above It All (Acoustic)" sung by The McClures, Bethel Moment

POUR OUT YOUR HEART

Write a prayer to God describing a situation in which you need victory. Ask Him to turn your heart toward Him in those moments so that you can rise above your fear.

EVENING PRAISE

Lord Jesus, as I close my day,

I once again praise You that You have already

accomplished the victory that is mine.

I praise You that You are now seated at the right hand of God,

the Father.

I exalt You that You live to intercede for me

in my battle against fear.

Thank You that You are for me and not against me.

I worship You because Your mercy and love envelop me.

I praise You because You are good in everything You do.

Thank You that I can trust You to defeat Satan

and any threat he brings to my life.

I rest protected by Your blood

and clothed in Your righteousness.

BASED ON 1 CORINTHIANS 15:5–7; MARK 16:19; ISAIAH 61:10; PSALM 62:1

WE CAN TRUST HIM FOR THE VICTORY

MORNING PRAYER

Lord Jesus, I long to live a life of victory today.

As I step into this new day,

fill me with Your Holy Spirit.

In the moments when I get discouraged,

remind me of Your promises.

I praise You that I can trust Your promises.

In the moments when

I feel afraid or anxious,

remind me of Your goodness.

I will sing to You today, Lord.

You are the one who gives victory.

BASED ON EPHESIANS 5:18; 2 CORINTHIANS 1:20; PSALM 31:19; 144:9–10

Yesterday, we studied the incredible story of the victory that the Lord won for Jehoshaphat and all of Judah. As the people marched out singing the praises of the Lord, the Lord sent ambushes and annihilated the enemies. We read that story and our faith is strengthened. But in a world filled with financial pressures, injustice, illness, and violence, it's easy to panic and feel anxious. How can we learn to trust God for victory in our lives? That's what we're going to study today.

Psalm 145 is an acrostic poem that contains twenty-two couplets, each beginning with successive letters of the Hebrew alphabet. It covers five different aspects of verbal praise: exalt, praise, proclaim, meditate, speak, celebrate, and sing. Go back through the psalm as if written out for you, and highlight each of those words. It also gives us five related keys to ongoing victory over anxiety.

EXPLORE

READ PSALM 145:1-2

KEY 1: Exalt and praise the Lord every day.

READ PSALM 145:3-4

List several of God's character traits in the space below that you could praise Him for day-by-day.

KEY 2: Meditate on His works.

What works has God accomplished in your life or in the life of someone you love recently? How might meditating on what God has accomplished fuel your praise life?

KEY 3: Proclaim His great deeds.

READ PSALM 145:6

What are some of the "great deeds" that God has accomplished through history? Can you list a few references of stories when God has accomplished a great deed? (Example: the crucifixion—Matthew 27:27–44)

KEY 4: Celebrate His abundant goodness.

READ PSALM 145:7–12

What evidence do you have of God's abundant goodness? How is God abundantly good to all mankind?

KEY 5: Focus on His faithful promises.

READ PSALM 145:13–20

List three promises of God with a reference for each one in the space below. If you can't remember where the verse is found that shares the promise, look the promise up online and it will give you the reference.

READ PSALM 145:21

Re-write the verse using your own words.

SELAH—PAUSE AND REFLECT

Spend a few minutes reflecting on the five keys to victory. Choose one and decide to start implementing it into your everyday life.

When you think of the word "exalt" that's used in Psalm 145:1, it reminds you to lift up and praise. How might praising lift up your own attitude?

As you consider the promises of God, what is one promise that is particularly precious to you personally? Write that promise in the space below.

MEMORIZE: Write out Psalm 68:26 in the space below.

LISTEN: "There's No Other Name (Acoustic)" sung by The McClures—Bethel Moment

POUR OUT YOUR HEART

Write a prayer to the Lord expressing your desire to live a life of ongoing praise day-by-day.

EVENING PRAISE

Lord Jesus, I praise You that victory belongs to You alone!

I thank You that You lead me in victory

as I continually praise and thank You for all You've done

in my life.

Thank You that You have promised me

that I can triumph over the enemy,

by Your blood and the word of my testimony.

I praise You that You are the King of kings

and the Lord of lords.

I praise You, Lord God Almighty, that You reign!

Thank You that I can trust You while I sleep.

BASED ON PSALM 3:3; 1 CORINTHIANS 15:57; REVELATION 12:11; 19:16

THE ONGOING CHALLENGE

MORNING PRAYER

Lord Jesus, I praise You this morning for who You are.
All glory, honor, wisdom, power, and blessing belong to You.
Worthy are You, Lord Jesus! You deserve all of my praise.
Lord, as I enter this new day,
I thank You that You have invited me to worship You.
I ask that You, Holy Spirit, would fill my heart with
thanksgiving and praise throughout my day.
I ask that Your praise would ever be on my lips.
Now that I am discovering the deep joy of praising You,
I pray that my life would be a continual offering of
never-ending praise!

BASED ON REVELATION 7:12; 5:12; PSALM 34:1

It's hard to believe that we are at the end of our six-week study. I hope you have fallen in love with the psalmists and their songs of praise. More than that, I hope you have become addicted to praise in your own spiritual journey. Praising God changes everything! As you continue on in your journey of praise, I believe your faith will be strengthened, your joy will increase, and your ability to hear God's voice and experience His presence will surge! Praise that is rooted in God's Word and focused on God's glory will unleash God's power in your life in ways you never expected. I believe as you continue, you will experience victory as never before!

As we spend eternity in God's presence we will be living in ceaseless praise. Here's the thing; eternity starts *now*. Make it your practice to live now like you will then. Psalm 150 is the perfect psalm to cultivate this practice.

EXPLORE

READ PSALM 150 OUT LOUD

What is the emotional tone of this psalm?

READ BACK THROUGH THE PSALM

Circle every instance of the word "praise."

This is a psalm of extreme and exuberant praise. There's no holding back here. The Hebrew word for praise that's used here is the word *halal* meaning "to shine boast, rave, and celebrate clamorously!" Friends, this is not quiet, mellow worship. This is loud, boisterous, exuberant, dancing-in-the-aisles type worship! Now, I'm just guessing here, but it's possible that it's been a long time since you've danced in the aisles.

Ask yourself: Has your worship become stale or flat? I mean, the psalmist is instructing us to exuberantly and enthusiastically praise God with loud instruments and shouts of joy! How do you feel about that? Consider that our worship is to be varied. There is a place for quiet, contemplative worship, and weeping worship, as well as loud, exuberant, boisterous worship! Praise comes in all different styles and sounds. The key is we are to set our focus on becoming true worshipers who are exuberant in our praise.

As my husband Steve and I have travelled to many different countries, we have been blessed by the colorful, exuberant worship. There's no embarrassment or shame as African women and men dance down the aisles as they worship with their offerings. We've watched children dance and wave flags of praise to the Lord in parts of Asia. I've had the privilege of worshiping with over 1,000 women in conferences in Latin America, and I've been humbled to watch over 6,000 women fill a stadium worshiping to "Great Is Thy Faithfulness" in Eastern Europe. All around the world, believers have learned the extraordinary power of praise.

READ THROUGH PSALM 150 AGAIN

Write down all the instruments mentioned.

READ PSALM 47:1

The Hebrew word for the word "clap" that's used here is *taqa*. It means "to clatter, clang, sound, blow (trumpets), clap, strike."[2] It implies energetic and enthusiastic praise!

How do you feel when a worship service is energetic and loud?

SELAH—PAUSE AND REFLECT

Do you prefer quiet and soft worship music or loud and vibrant worship music?

Whichever your preference, what would be the benefit to your worship for you to embrace both quiet reflective worship as well as loud and exuberant worship?

What has been your main takeaway from this Bible study?

What have you learned about yourself through this study?

What have you learned about God through your study of the Psalms?

MEMORIZE: Write out Psalm 68:26 from memory.

LISTEN: "Echo Holy, Now (Here)" performed by Red Rocks Worship

POUR OUT YOUR HEART

In the space provided below write out a prayer to the Lord expressing your desire for a deeper worship walk.

EVENING PRAISE

Praise You, Lord.

Praise the Lord, my soul.

Help me to praise You, Lord, for all of my life.

Oh Father, I praise and thank You for all

I have learned through this study.

I praise You that You are worthy of my unhindered praise.

Holy Spirit, I pray that You would unleash my tongue to

praise You more.

Let me live in unceasing praise.

Oh Lord, You are worthy to receive

power and wealth and wisdom and strength

and honor and glory and praise!

BASED ON PSALM 146:1-2; REVELATION 5:12

A REVIEW OF PRACTICES TO STRENGTHEN
YOUR PRAISE JOURNEY

Through this study we've looked at several worship practices that might be new to you. Each practice will quiet your anxiety, enhance your praise journey, and strengthen your walk with the Lord. I thought it would be helpful for you to have a list of ten worship practices we looked at through this study.

1. **Getting on your knees and listening to worship music.** Allow the music to prompt your praise. (I have literally begun my day like this for the last twenty years, and it has radically changed my life.)

2. **Journaling your prayers.** The psalmists poured out their hearts before the Lord. One tangible way to do this is to adopt the practice of journaling your thoughts as prayers to the Lord every day.

3. **Thanking the Lord for His love every morning and His faithfulness every evening.** Wrapping your day in praise and thanksgiving will fill your heart with more peace than you can imagine.

4. **Reading a psalm out loud.** Often when we read silently our minds wander, so try reading a psalm out loud as part of your worship journey.

5. **Sitting in silence before the Lord.** My recommendation is that you begin with 2–3 minutes every morning of being still before the Lord. Keep your mind focused on one character trait of the Lord, and simply enjoy His presence.

6. **Weeping and lamenting before the Lord.** Remember, worship is not always all "happy clappy." Tears shed in worship before the Lord have an honored place in His heart.

7. **Creating a thankful list.** Writing down the top three blessings of every day will enlarge your heart to hold more gratefulness.

8. **Raising your hands in worship.** You can do this in the privacy of your own home or gathered with others to worship. Remember, raising your hands is the universal sign of surrender.

9. **Dancing before the Lord in celebration.** This might be a stretch for you, but you might try this at home. God loves our undignified raw worship.

10. **Praying Scripture back to God.** God is delighted with His word. When you claim His promises and pray His words back to Him, the Holy Spirit uses those words to strengthen your faith and delight God's heart.

GLOSSARY OF HEBREW WORDS
(PRAISE AND WORSHIP)

Hello, friend, I thought it might be helpful for you to have a glossary of Hebrew words related to praise and worship all in one place. You can check back here as you continue your ongoing journey into the Psalms.

Abad (Strong's Concordance #5647) "To work for, serve, do labor for someone; to be a servant; to worship." Used in Psalm 100:2: "Worship the LORD with gladness; come before him with joyful songs."

Barach (Strong's Concordance #1288) "To bless; to salute, congratulate, thank, praise, to kneel down." Used in Psalm 145:2: "Every day I will praise you and extol your name for ever and ever." (Also, Psalm 95:6; 34:1.)

Halal (Strong's Concordance #1984) "To shine, boast, rave, and celebrate clamorously." The word carries the idea of triumph. It speaks to expressive, exuberant, loud praise! This is the primary Hebrew word used for praise. It is the word from which we get "Hallelujah." Used in Psalm 150:2: "Praise him for his acts of power; praise him for his surpassing greatness."

Mizmor (Strong's Concordance #4210a) The word "psalm," or *mizmor* in Hebrew, means "an instrumental song, a song accompanied by musical instruments." (Used throughout the Psalms.)

Shabach (Strong's Concordance #7623) "To bow down as an act of submission or reverence." The primary meaning is "to make oneself low." Used in Psalm 99:5: "Exalt the LORD our God and worship at his footstool; he is holy." (Also, Psalms 47:1; 145:4.)

Tehillah (Strong's Concordance #8416) "A celebration, a lauding of someone praiseworthy; the praise or exaltation of God; praises, songs of admiration." Used in Psalm 100:4: "Enter his gates with thanksgiving and his courts with praise." (Also, Psalm 22:3.)

Yadah (Strong's Concordance #3034) "To throw or cast or the extended hand, as in the giving of thanks." Used in Psalm 107:15: "Let them give thanks to the LORD for his unfailing love and his wonderful deeds for mankind." (Also, Psalm 43:4; 138:4.)

Zamar (Strong's Concordance #2167) "To make music, sing praises; to sing songs accompanied by musical instruments." Used in Psalm 149:3: "Let them praise his name with dancing and make music to him with timbrel and harp." (Also, Psalms 21:13; 57:8–9.)

LISTENING GUIDE FOR VIDEO TEACHING

SESSION 1 | FACING YOUR FEARS

> *"The LORD is my light and my salvation—*
> *whom shall I fear?*
> *The LORD is the stronghold of my life—*
> *of whom shall I be afraid?"*
>
> PSALM 27:1

The psalmist David wrestled with the emotions we face today, including anxiety (see Psalm 94:18–19).

Who or what is your Goliath now? What is the taunt of your Goliath?

David struggled with anxiety and fear, but his inner life prepared him for life and for the threats he would face.

David adopted a rhythm that we can follow:
David poured out his heart in authenticity before God. Then he would refocus on the Lord and bring it back to praise.

THE PSALMS SHOW US:

1. The strength of your inner life is going to determine your courage and calm when adversity comes.

2. The time spent on your knees, pouring out your heart to the King of kings and Lord of lords—that's not wasted time.

3. Your authenticity before God is going to determine your intimacy with God.

4. The Psalms teach us of the magnificence of the God we serve.

SESSION 2 | HOW LONG, LORD?

"How long, Lord? Will you forget me forever?
How long will you hide your face from me?
How long must I wrestle with my thoughts
and day after day have sorrow in my heart?"

PSALM 13:1

Waiting is a key discipleship issue for every believer. If we don't learn how to wait in the presence of the Lord, God won't use us to accomplish what He wants to do in and through us. God will call us to wait, just like He often did with David.

DAVID'S EXAMPLE

Psalm 13:1 shows us David is wrestling in his heart when God calls him to wait.

David had to wait to become king because of Saul's jealousy.

"Jealousy turns our heart toward insanity. If you allow jealousy to take root in your heart and you don't uproot it, it will distort your thinking and you will end up becoming paranoid."

IN THE WAITING

1. Waiting is an invitation to embrace our human limitations.

2. Waiting is an invitation to surrender control to God's timing.

3. Waiting is an invitation to increase our humility.

    God can't do anything in us or through us if pride is in the way.
    When we are waiting, God does a reformation of our soul and develops humility in us so we become more like Jesus.

4. Waiting is an invitation to enlarge our heart to hold the platform that God wants to give us.

5. Waiting is an invitation to deepen our desire for the Giver of the gifts rather than the gift itself.

LET'S LINGER AND WAIT IN GOD'S PRESENCE!

SESSION 3 | THE TREASURE OF LAMENTING

With my mouth I will greatly extol the LORD;
in the great throng of worshipers I will praise him.
For he stands at the right hand of the needy,
to save their lives from those who would condemn them.

PSALM 109:30–31

Weeping has an honored place in the life of believers. Lament is where we cry out before God and we wrestle with Him. We may weep and we may question God. We are called to be like Jesus who wept in sorrow and showed emotions.

> Jesus wept — John 11:35
>
> Jesus felt angry — Mark 3:5
>
> Jesus was overwhelmed with sorrow — Matthew 26:38

It was never God's idea for us to numb our feelings.

LAMENTING PSALMS—"IMPRECATORY" PSALMS

"My God, whom I praise, do not remain silent, for people who are wicked and deceitful have opened their mouths against me; they have spoken against me with lying tongues." (Psalm 109:1–2)

HOW TO SEE ANGER

Anger is a secondary emotion and often comes as a result of other emotions, such as sorrow and grief.

Look at the story of David, Nabal, and Abigail as told in 1 Samuel 25:24–29.

1. **See Your Anger as a Signal that Your Soul Needs Attention**

   When angry, pause and have a "self-management meeting,"
   asking, *What is in my soul that needs attention?*

2. See your anger as a tool. It can be for construction or for destruction.

3. See your anger as an opportunity to look for God's provision.

4. See your anger as an invitation to trust God with justice.

Create space alone with God. Ask Him, "What do You want to speak to me about my anger?"

SESSION 4 | CONTENTMENT WHEN GOD SAYS NO

Then King David went in and sat before the LORD . . .

2 SAMUEL 7:18

God calls us to worship Him and find the place of contentment, which is difficult when God says no.

See 2 Samuel 7—David's dream was to build a temple for the LORD. Though God says no to David, He doesn't leave him there. He tells David:

"I will make your name great." (v. 9)
"I will provide a place for my people." (v. 10)
"I will give you rest from all your enemies." (v. 11)
"I will raise up your offspring. . . . [your son] will build a house for my Name." (vv. 12–13)

DAVID'S RESPONSE WHEN GOD SAID NO:

1. DAVID SAT BEFORE THE LORD

"Then King David went in and sat before the LORD . . ." (2 Samuel 7:18)

How do you respond when God says no?

1 Timothy 6:6 — "But godliness with contentment is great gain."

2. DAVID DIDN'T JUST SIT THERE—HE WORSHIPED GOD

- David worships God in the moment that God says no (see 2 Samuel 7:18–24).
- Contentment is finding rest through worshiping God when He says no.
- Contentment is leaning back into the Almighty and saying, "You know what's best."

3. DAVID CHOSE TO NURTURE A STATE OF CONTENTMENT IN HIS SOUL:

- He chose to worship when he could have raised his fist.
- He looked back and remembered what God had done.
- He nurtured an attitude of gratitude.
- He always created space to worship the wonder of God, and never lost his sense of wonder.

What does it look like to create the space in your life to recapture a sense of wonder?

Contentment is the worship that springs from resting in God . . . even when He says no.

SESSION 5 | PRAISE RESTORES JOY

"The Lord has done great things for us,

and we are filled with joy."

PSALM 126:3

PURE WORSHIP DELIGHTS THE HEART OF GOD

David's example in 2 Samuel 6 — "I will celebrate before the Lord" (v. 21).

THE EXTRAORDINARY POWER OF PRAISE IS THAT:

1. WORSHIP RESTORES LOST JOY

- Psalm 16:11—"You make known to me the path of life; you will fill me with joy in your presence, with eternal pleasures at your right hand."

- Pure worship delights the heart of God

2. WORSHIP HELPS US FEEL GOD'S PRESENCE AND MORE CONNECTED TO HIM

3. WORSHIP TRANSFORMS US INTO THE IMAGE OF GOD

- God is the joy giver. As you worship and praise Him, you are transformed into the image of His Son.

- Psalm 34:5—"Those who look to him are radiant; their faces are never covered with shame."
- Psalm 34:1—"I will extol the Lord at all times; his praise will always be on my lips."

SESSION 6 | RHYTHMS OF ONGOING VICTORY

It is good to praise the LORD and make music
to your name, O Most High, proclaiming your love
in the morning and your faithfulness at night.

PSALM 92:1-2

"The LORD gave David victory wherever he went." (2 Samuel 8:6b)

David didn't live a perfect life, but God gave him victory wherever he went. For the psalmist, victory is a rhythm of life.

Set Rhythms of Praise in Your Life—What does that look like?

THREE INVITATIONS TO HELP YOU CRAFT A LIFE OF PRAISE BASED ON PSALM 95

1. COME BEFORE GOD AND PRAISE HIM FOR HIS CHARACTER

"Come, let us sing for joy to the LORD; let us shout aloud to the Rock of our salvation." (Psalm 95:1)

2. REMEMBER THE GOODNESS OF THE LORD AND GIVE HIM THANKS

"Let us come before him with thanksgiving and extol him with music and song." (Psalm 95:2)

3. MAINTAIN A POSITION OF ONGOING SURRENDER

"Come, let us bow down in worship, let us kneel before the LORD our Maker; for he is our God and we are the people of his pasture, the flock under his care." (Psalm 95:6–7)

The Extraordinary Power of Praise **is that as you faithfully practice praising Him, He is going to change you! Make this pattern of praise your new normal.**

ACKNOWLEDGMENTS

SPECIAL THANKS TO:

MY HUSBAND, STEVE—

Babe, I love how we can process ideas together and give input to each other as we write and speak. Thank you for always believing in me and supporting the ministry God has called me to. I love you!

MY KIDS AND KIDS-IN-LOVE—

Bethany and Chris. You guys are amazing. I love the way you are raising five boys to know and love Jesus and to be men of integrity. I love your hearts for kiddos in foster care and for supporting parents who have adopted. I love you both tons!

Josiah and Shaina. I love how supportive you two are of Dad and me in our ministries. And both of your hearts for prayer! JJ, watching you and Dad launch the new mission, Compel Global, has been extraordinary. What a joy to be able to do ministry with you! I love you both tons!

Stefanie and Dave. I love how you guys have such a heart for emotionally healthy discipleship. Watching you lead Alpha groups, as well as actively discipling others, has been such a joy! I love you both tons!

Keri and Zach. Oh, what a joy to watch both of your hearts for worship and praise and leading others toward Christ. I love the way you both love others and are continually reaching out to neighbors and friends with encouragement. You are both extraordinary! I love you both tons!

MY GRANDKIDS!—

Charlie, Ty, Joshua, Selah, Zachary, Theo, Noah, Rayna, Cayden, Kinley, Tori, Melody, Asher, and Austin! Wow! You guys fill this Mimi's heart with so much joy. Watching you growing in your love for Jesus and learning how to serve Him fills my heart with more joy than you can imagine. I pray all of you continue to grow up loving Him and praising Him! I love you all tons!

MY AGENT AND TREASURED FRIEND, BLYTHE DANIELS—

Blythe, in addition to being my agent, you are such a dear friend! I love your heart for prayer and your heart to get the Word into people's lives! Love you!

ALL THE MEN AND WOMEN FROM MOODY PUBLISHERS—

Judy Dunagan. Ah, Judy, in addition to being my acquisitions editor, you are my dear friend. I treasure our times together. Whether we're praying together on our knees or laughing hysterically over coffee, I am so beyond blessed by you! Love you, dear friend!

My amazing intern, Tiffany Curtis. Oh, Tiffany, what a joy to work with you and see you grow into such a phenomenal editor! I love you and appreciate you so much!

My amazing editor, Amanda Cleary Eastep. What a joy to work with you, Amanda. I love your heart for detail and definitely couldn't do this without you. Thank you for your patient efforts in working with me on this project! Love you, Amanda!

My precious friend and mentor, Linda Dillow, who first challenged me to praise God even during the darkest moments of my life. I love you!

NOTES

INTRODUCTION

1. Dan Allender and Tremper Longman III, *The Cry of the Soul: How Our Emotions Reveal Our Deepest Questions about God* (Colorado Springs, CO: NavPress, 1994), 20.

2. "Find Help for Women and Anxiety," Anxiety and Depression Association of America, https://adaa.org/find-help-for/women/anxiety.

3. "Mizmor," Strong's Concordance #4210a, https://www.biblestudytools.com/concordances/strongs-exhaustive-concordance.

WEEK 1 | FACING YOUR FEARS

1. Lily Rothman, "Why Americans Are More Afraid Than They Used to Be," *Time*, January 6, 2016, http://time.com/4158007/american-fear-history.

2. "Shadday," Strong's Concordance #7706.

3. "Elyon," Strong's Concordance #5946.

4. "Elohim," Strong's Concordance #430.

5. "Fowler," Bible Study Tools, https://www.biblestudytools.com/dictionary/fowler.

6. "Which Psalms Predict the Coming of Jesus Christ?," Got Questions, https://www.gotquestions.org/Psalms-Jesus-Christ.html.

7. "Yhvh" (Yahweh), Strong's Concordance #3068.

8. "Adonay" (Adonai), Strong's Concordance #136.

9. Jack Hayford, gen. ed., *The Spirit Filled Life Bible* (Nashville: Thomas Nelson, 2014), study notes.

WEEK 2 | WAITING WHILE YOU WORSHIP

1. Eugene H. Peterson, *The Jesus Way: A Conversation on the Ways That Jesus Is the Way* (Grand Rapids, MI: Eerdmans, 2007), 97.

2. V. Raymond Edman, *The Disciplines of Life* (Wheaton, IL: Victor, 1948), 80.

3. Bob Sorge, *The Fire of Delayed Answers: Are You Waiting for Your Prayers to Be Answered?* (Greenwood, MS: Oasis House, 1996), 61.

4. Dr. and Mrs. Howard Taylor, *Hudson Taylor's Spiritual Secret* (London: China Inland Mission, 1935), 75.

5. Andrew Murray, *Waiting on God* (Springdale, PA: Whitaker House, 1981), 49.

6. "Psalm 37:4," Bible Hub, https://biblehub.com/lexicon/psalms/37-4.htm.

7. "Heart," Strong's Concordance #3820.

8. C. H. Spurgeon, *The Treasury of David*, vol.1 (McLean, VA: MacDonald Publishing Company, n.d.), 171.

9. "Prayer of Saint Teresa of Avila," EWTN, https://www.ewtn.com/catholicism/devotions/prayer-of-saint-teresa-of-avila-364.

10. Eugene H. Peterson, *Leap Over a Wall: Earthly Spirituality for Everyday Christians* (San Francisco: HarperCollins, 1997), 162–63.

11. Murray, *Waiting on God*, 52.

12. Pete Greig, *Dirty Glory: Go Where Your Best Prayers Take You* (Colorado Springs, CO: NavPress, 2016), 46.

13. Biography of Rev. Duncan Campbell, Sermon Audio, https://www.sermonaudio.com/search.asp?speakeronly=true&currsection=sermonsspeaker&keyword=Rev._Duncan_Campbell.

14. Duncan Campbell, quoted in "Theology of Revival," https://sbts-wordpress-uploads.s3.amazonaws.com/equip/uploads/2009/09/revival-handout.pdf.

WEEK 3 | LAMENTING WITH AUTHENTICITY

1. Dan Allender and Tremper Longman III, *The Cry of the Soul: How Our Emotions Reveal Our Deepest Questions about God* (Colorado Springs, CO: NavPress, 1994), 19.

2. "Sustain," Strong's Concordance #3557.

3. Peter Scazzero, *Emotionally Healthy Relationships Day by Day: A 40-Day Journey to Deeply Change Your Relationships* (Grand Rapids, MI: Zondervan, 2017), 195.

4. Michael Card, *A Sacred Sorrow: Reaching Out to God in the Lost Language of Lament* (Colorado Springs, CO: NavPress, 2005), 21.

5. Scazzero, *Emotionally Healthy Relationships Day by Day*, 125.

6. Card, *A Sacred Sorrow*, 77.

7. "*Hyssopus officinalis*," Wikipedia, last edited on December 23, 2020, https://en.wikipedia.org/wiki/Hyssopus_officinalis.